W9-APP-032

APR. 2 7 1996
JUN. 2 0 1996

B
Root   Root, Eric

        Lana: The private
        diary of my life

DEMCO

The Private Diary of My Life With

Lana

The Private Diary of My Life With Lana

by ERIC ROOT

with Dale Crawford
and Raymond Strait

DOVE
BOOKS

Copyright © 1996 by Dove Audio, Inc.

All rights reserved. No part of this book may be reproduced or transmitted in any form or by any means, electronic or mechanical, including photocopying, recording, or by any information storage and retrieval system, without permission in writing from the publisher.

ISBN 0-7871-0773-5

Printed in the United States of America

Dove Books
301 North Cañon Drive
Beverly Hills, CA 90210

Distributed by Penguin USA

Text design and layout by Stanley S. Drate/Folio Graphics Co. Inc.
Jacket design and layout by Rick Penn-Kraus
Photo insert by Mauna Eichner

The author wishes to thank Bob Scott for use of the cover photo, and several photos in the insert.

First Printing: February 1996

10 9 8 7 6 5 4 3 2 1

For my mother,
who has given me the love,
understanding, and encouragement
to pursue this project

God, teach me to guard my mouth and let only
truth come out of it. Since truth cannot
be changed, truth that I speak can change the world.

Acknowledgments

At Dove: Michael Viner, Mary Aarons, Mauna Eichner, Doug Field, Lee Fukui, Jacquie Melnick, Lee Montgomery, Marie Rowe, Stefan Rudnicki, Wendy Walker, Michele Samat, Shauna Zurbrugg.

And: Jules Aaron, Chris and Peri Alcaid, June Allyson, Peter Aynsley, Charif Bassiouni, Katia Beebe, Turhan Bey, Bing Bruce, Linda Christian, Susan Cowen, Carmen Cruz, Deborah Devine, Francis Diaz, Yossi Dina, Tim James, Gregg Juarez, Yiannis Karimalis, Morgana King, Karen Kondazian, Shirley O'Hara Krims, Bessie Little, Gloria Luckenbill, Jan Moran, Debbie Reynolds, Hal and Sylvia Rhodes, Harriet Root, Mrs. Anwar Sadat, Ron Schneider, Guadalupe Shannon, Aly Spencer, Edward and Debbie Stavitsky, Lou Valentino, Jack Vizzard, Raquel Welch, Dorothy Davis, Marvin Page, Robin Leach, Kenneth and Diane Wittstock.

Special thanks following Lana's death for the support of my family, friends, and especially Carmencita.

Thanks to Raymond Strait for his professionalism and ability to meet a deadline. Thanks to Dale Crawford for starting the journey.

Posthumously: Rupert Allen, Lucille Ball, Anne Baxter, Richard Burton, Valerie Douglas, Sir Laurence Olivier, Johnny Ray, Ginger Rogers, and Sammy Davis, Jr.

Contents

The Private Diary
of My Life With

Lana

Introduction

*L*ana died in the evening, on Tuesday, June 27, 1995. I was probably among the last to find out. No one from "the family," of which I had been an innermost member for the past twenty-five years, had even bothered to call and tell me the news. I didn't hear about her death until the next day.

I was relaxing at my home in Pacific Palisades, having spent the previous night driving back to Los Angeles after a long day at my salon near Palm Springs. I hadn't listened to a radio or been near a television set for the past twenty-four hours.

Late Wednesday morning my phone rang.

"Hello, Eric?" It was my friend Gloria Luckenbill.

I greeted her with an exuberant "Hello!"

"Eric, you sound so *up*."

"I *am* up," I replied. "It's a beautiful day out here away from smoggy L.A. and I feel great."

"Then you haven't heard?"

"Heard what?" I asked.

"Lana died."

I didn't get it. Those two simple words—direct words—just didn't compute with me. I thought I must not have heard her correctly.

"What?" I said, obviously confused.

"Lana died," she repeated.

"WHAT?!" I shouted. "Oh God, no . . ."

A quick chill followed by a wave of nausea shot through my entire body like high voltage, causing me to shudder.

"When?" I asked, my stomach churning.

"Last night, around 8 P.M.," she replied.

I don't remember anything we said after that. My senses reeled as shock and disbelief set in. Somewhere inside me floodgates of grief were opening up. In a matter of seconds my breath came in spurts and I began to cry softly. Lana, my Lana . . . my beloved "little sister," my compatriot queen, my devil's advocate, my friend . . .

Of course, I'd known for some time the seriousness of her illness. Anyone reading the tabloids knew that much. From time to time mutual friends had passed along bits of information. Even a confidential source at Cedars-Sinai Medical Center, where she had been receiving chemotherapy and radiation treatments, had recently told me her prognosis should be considered short rather than long-term. But I reasoned that in Hollywood the fine line between gossip and reality was often blurred.

Lana the invincible, a woman capable of prevailing against insurmountable odds. The world knew that. Hadn't she just returned from Spain, where she'd received an award from the Spanish Film Industry? Hadn't certain people, who should have known, assured me unequivocally that her cancer was in remission?

I guess it is true we believe what we want to believe and simply rationalize away unpleasant realities.

Spinning from the shock of her death, I canceled my afternoon appointments, spoke with a few close friends by phone, and spent the rest of the day in a fog. At midday I found myself at the beach meditating, praying for both Lana and the strength to get through one of the greatest tragedies of my life.

I hadn't begun to comprehend the enormity of my loss and the effect it would have on my life. It was inconceivable that she was gone, that I would never see her again, never be able to repair the recent, inexplicable breach between us. I had a right to say good-bye.

I passed a newsstand later in the afternoon. Photos of Lana and stories of her death—most of them prepared well in advance—were splashed across the front pages of every major newspaper, to be followed—in a matter of days—by reports in the weekly tabloids and news magazines.

The international press also gave her death front-page coverage, such was her notoriety and the worldwide impact of her films for nearly half a century. Lana, never lacking in self-importance, would have understood this phenomenon and probably enjoyed it.

By the time I returned home and turned on my television, Lana's death was the lead story on every channel. The coverage reached its peak with retrospectives on cable as well as network news programs. Leonard Maltin delivered a lengthy tribute on "Entertainment Tonight." Timeless images of a young Lana Turner were flashed around the globe—via *instantaneous* satellite—everywhere at once in a blazing finale. I watched for a few minutes, then quietly pressed the remote and silenced the screen, unable to bear more.

Even as the eulogies and tributes to Lana poured in from around the world, another movie star incident in Los Angeles also grabbed world headlines—threatening to "upstage" her exit. Actor Hugh Grant had been arrested while having sex with a prostitute in his car and quickly found himself enmeshed in a scandal that would generate copy for weeks to come. (Instead of destroying his career, as it would have during Lana's time, the incident hyped ticket sales for his soon-to-be-released film. Go figure!)

These two seemingly unconnected events shared the celebrity spotlight over the weekend of June 30, 1995, and more than one astute commentator linked them, noting that headlines from Lana's scandal-ridden past made the Grant affair look like an afternoon walk in the park. They were referring, of course, to one event in particular.

In 1958 Lana had been the center of one of the biggest and juiciest murder scandals in Hollywood history—the still questionable murder of her gangster boyfriend, Johnny Stompanato—to which her fourteen-year-old daughter confessed.

At the time Lana was in the midst of making a comeback, having just received an Oscar nomination for Best Actress for her role in the sizzling *Peyton Place* (in which a young girl murders her rapist stepfather). She suddenly found herself facing a hostile press and public condemnation so potentially damaging it might have meant an end to her career.

It is more than a small tribute to Lana's innate sense of survival that she used her considerable wealth, power, and connections to manipulate the circumstances of her destruction and emerge the victor. Her next film, *Imitation Of Life*, in which she played an actress in love with the same man as her daughter, would become the biggest success of her long career. One wonders where life ends and art reflects.

In the days and weeks following Lana's death, I missed her beyond belief. I found it impossible to overestimate the role she'd played in my life. Every place I looked, every drawer I opened revealed some precious memory. The ghosts were everywhere—in framed photos hanging on the walls of my salons, in my appointment books and journals, in dozens of personal notes she'd written me and a thousand candid snapshots from our travels. I would come to understand I possessed photos and text that comprised a unique, multifaceted diary of our life together.

I recall a night, ten years earlier, in her suite at The Plaza Hotel in New York City. At three in the morning we were sitting around talking and drinking after a particularly exhilarating evening. A news documentary on television droned on, the volume low, about some long-forgotten Hollywood scandal when suddenly Johnny Stompanato's face filled the screen, followed by the world-famous image of Lana on the witness stand during the inquest. Across the room I saw Lana's body visibly stiffen. She placed her glass of wine down on the coffee table firmly.

"Lana," I asked, "do you want me to shut it off?"

"No," she said resolutely, taking the remote and increasing the volume as she listened and watched intently. Finally, when the narrator went on to something else, she clicked off the set, as though she could actually erase the images in her head forever. It seemed an eternity before she spoke.

"Tell it," she said, looking me straight in the eye. "Tell the truth . . . someday . . . when I'm gone . . . tell it all, Eric. . . ."

~ 1 ~

Eulogy

LOS ANGELES, EARLY JULY 1995

$\mathscr{I}$ met Lana Turner in 1971, and for nearly a quarter of a century hardly a day went by when we weren't together or in constant touch by phone. I spent more time with her than did any of her husbands, lovers, directors, costars, agents, managers, secretaries, or even her daughter, Cheryl. Only two people spent more time with her during those years: her maid, Carmen, and her mother, Mildred.

I always considered it a pleasure to be not only her hairdresser but her spiritual brother, friend, consort, escort, protector, and confidant. Conversely, I knew the pain and aggravation of becoming her sounding board, hatchet man, negotiator, spokesperson, and go-between, as well as last-minute substitute whenever she canceled an appearance.

To call our relationship a mixture of heaven and hell would be a monumental understatement. Lana was an indisputable star of superior magnitude, one

of the great screen beauties of all time, and as anyone who ever knew her could attest, heavenly she
was and hell she could be. . . .

*W*hen Lana died of throat cancer in her Century
City high-rise condo (her "Ivory Tower," she called
it), her passing marked not only the end of an era
but also the extinction of a unique Hollywood spe-
cies: the Love Goddess. Nurtured, groomed, and protected by a once-powerful studio contract system,
Lana and her famous contemporaries—Rita Hayworth, Betty Grable, Elizabeth Taylor, and later
Marilyn Monroe and Grace Kelly—became superstars, the pinup queens and glamour girls of both
World War II and the post-World War II generation.
On-screen and off they remained among the world's
most publicized, photographed, and desirable
women for several decades past their prime.

By the late 1980s times had changed. Most of her
contemporaries were gone, casualties of life on the
Hollywood fast track and ever-changing public
tastes. Lana was in reluctant retirement, and with
the possible exception of Elizabeth Taylor, few of the
Love Goddesses were working. The system and cli-
mate that had created them had been dismantled.
Idealized beauty and a sense of things better left to
the imagination were lost to antiquity, replaced by
explicit, in-your-face sexuality. Flawless creatures
who merely suggested the mystery and promise of
sex had become passé.

Frustrated by rapid changes within the film industry and her inability to stop the clock, Lana began working less (despite making several important television guest appearances) and drinking more, spending most of her time behind the doors of her "Ivory Tower." Only an occasional awards ceremony, preferably one at which she would be the guest of honor, could lure her out from her Century City penthouse.

More and more frequently she was a no-show at functions she had committed to attend, often sending me in her place to offer her excuses and apologies and to soothe her angry hosts. Sadly, the results of these failures would further tarnish her standing within the film colony, adding an illusive but ultimately damaging footnote to her reputation. To totally blame her later behavior on pure selfishness would be a mistake.

Vanity became her biggest problem and her deepest flaw. The ravages of time and hard living were taking their toll and, after so many years of recognition for her incredible beauty and glamour, she found it increasingly difficult to face her public.

On numerous occasions we would be dressed to go out for the evening, only to be stopped by the mirror hanging like a sentinel in her entryway—the final checkpoint. Having already changed her gown or her jewelry six or seven times, she would look gorgeous as we headed for the door. But in the pit of my stomach I knew we still had to pass inspection in front of that damn mirror. I could read her like a book. If she didn't like what she saw (she was terrified she didn't look as good as people expected), we would not be going out. Instead, we'd find ourselves propped up in her bed watching television—again.

"Darling, I just can't," she would say, almost in tears. "It's my diarrhea (her most common manifestation of nerves), and I'm just not going to be able to make it. You go. Take the limo and go. . . ."

Ultimately, I believe she became a hostage to images of her younger self, breathtaking images from films constantly resurfacing on television. Her toughest competition would always be herself, and how could anyone compete with that?

At age seventy-four, Lana had been the last and, arguably, the most important star of her kind; the supreme, surviving femme fatale of a mythical Golden Age. Acknowledged even by her numerous detractors as one of the most beautiful women of the twentieth century, almost fifty years of stardom and scandal assured her a place of honor in the realm of legend and myth. For almost half those years we shared a loving, exasperating, and often stormy relationship. We were constant and closest companions. I shall miss her forever.

~✦ 2 ✦~

Access Denied

$\mathcal{D}$uring the final months of Lana's life, and when I should have been there—when she needed me most—the doors were slammed shut in my face. I didn't even learn about the memorial service until after the fact.

Less than a year earlier, when the doctors informed Lana the throat cancer she thought had been cured had returned, the "protectors" of her legacy circled the wagons around her. I found myself being systematically eliminated from her life.

Lana had never refused my phone calls, even when she had reason to be angry with me. Now she was "indisposed." Next, her private number was changed and the new one never given to me. The doormen at her building informed me that no one other than immediate family and doctors would be admitted.

I was calm at first as I attempted to absorb so

many dramatic changes. Then anger and frustration replaced my serenity. Every day brought some new roadblock. My major concern was Lana's health, as her day-to-day status became the object of changing rumors and speculation.

No matter how grave her illness was, her publicity remained decidedly upbeat. Liz Smith, the internationally syndicated columnist, wrote about her frequently. Press releases indicated she would soon be traveling to Europe to receive prestigious awards for her contribution to world cinema. I knew for a fact she had been making phone calls to a number of our mutual friends. Confused, I felt certain she would want to at least *talk* to me, her "beloved brother" with whom she had shared so many years, so many adventures.

My only access came through either Cheryl or Cheryl's lover, Josh, which meant *no* access. The couple *told* me that my letters and phone messages would be relayed, but were they? Cheryl and Josh declared their love for me, said they missed me, and were genuinely *sorry* about any recent *difficulties* between Lana and myself. Reliable sources confided that my flowers, Lana's favorite tuberoses, were delivered to her apartment on her birthday. I later discovered that she never received them.

The doors, slowly but surely, were creaking shut. I refused to believe it could happen, but my ties to Lana were severed. Completely and irrevocably.

In due time the final disrespect came. I had

expected it. I'd been removed from Lana's will. This action had taken place when Lana was facing her final battle for survival under what must have been an incoherent haze of medication, chemotherapy, and radiation. My only solace came in words so many of my friends had tried to drill into my head for several years: Blood is the only tie that counts.

Within a few days of Lana's passing, I received several hundred cards, letters, and phone calls of sympathy. Everyone knew I was "a member of the family." Friends and celebrities who had known us as a couple on the social circuit tried to console me in my grief. Their thoughtfulness and concern comforted me.

After a few weeks my thoughts turned to Cheryl. On her birthday, pride or no pride, I called to personally express my sorrow over her loss—our loss. Surely, at such a time, we were kindred spirits. "Cheryl, I just wanted to call to say how sorry I am," I said. "I know you're grieving, as I'm grieving. I miss your mother so much. I'm also calling to wish you happy birthday. . . ."

She didn't pick up the phone, nor did she return my call. I left my condolences on her answering machine, so I know she received them.

A week later, exactly one month to the day after Lana's death, I received an envelope in the mail addressed in Cheryl's handwriting. Finally, a message from Cheryl to her "Uncle Eric" (her nickname for me and a reference to the fact that Lana always called me her "brother"). But the envelope contained no such personal message, no expression of commiseration, no handwritten message—just a lovely 5x7, semiglossy, cream-colored card featuring one of Lana's most breathtaking MGM portraits, circa 1946.

It reminded me of the "fan card" publicity stills the studios used to send out to fans by the thousands, with one exception: The impersonal message below the photo read:

THE FAMILY OF LANA TURNER
WISH TO THANK YOU
FOR YOUR KIND EXPRESSION OF SYMPATHY

I found that cold, formal message from Cheryl a stark contrast from the message she personally inscribed to me on the flyleaf of her book, *Detour*:

To Uncle Eric —
What can I write that would pass the censors?
But you know I adore you.
Cheryl Crane

3

San Sebastian, Spain

SEPTEMBER 1994

I last saw Lana alive on television, on the show "Runaway with the Rich and Famous." Our friend Robin Leach had followed Lana with his cameras to Spain (as he had done when we went to Egypt ten years earlier) for what would be her last public appearance. The prestigious San Sebastian Film Festival was honoring her with a special Lifetime Achievement Award from the Spanish film industry. It surely took every ounce of her remaining stamina to do it, but my contacts in Spain tell me she exerted tremendous energy and determination. She wanted the world to know that any presumptions of her demise were highly exaggerated.

There was an irony. She had been invited to receive this same award back in 1988. I, of course, would accompany her. We were gearing up for the grand affair, agreeing that Lana's presence in the "star spot" would be a good career move. The award brought with it considerable and enticing perks: $10,000 fee (Lana negotiated for $15,000), first-class air and luxury hotel accommodations, plus—a big plus—an incredible amount of international press coverage.

Lana procrastinated for weeks but finally gave the festival organizers a verbal assurance of her attendance. Our passports were renewed and an itinerary carefully scheduled. Suddenly she decided to cancel the trip.

Again the hosts were left in the lurch, scrambling to find another suitable recipient at the last minute. It's a wonder and tribute to her everlasting movie star charisma that they invited her back.

In late September 1994 she arrived in Spain to collect her award. On the evening of the ceremony she was escorted from the Royal Suite of the historical Maria Christina Hotel and assisted into a convertible limousine. She received a thunderous ovation as she rode past thousands of fans lining the route to the Festival Theater.

I watched the event on television, both alarmed and saddened. Despite the hoopla of how wonderful she looked, I saw before me a frail, eighty-five pound woman, bejeweled and expensively gowned, standing alone on the theater's grand staircase in agony, trying to preserve her presence as a reigning cinema queen, par excellence.

I'd made that face up a thousand times. I knew her face like the back of my hand. I saw a tired, ill dowager queen, gaunt and haggard under too many coats of paint. The luminous, pearl-blond hair color I'd created to be her signature shade for the past twenty years was now, inexplicably, a drab ash brown, harsh and unflattering to her face, devoid of softening highlights for the camera to illuminate.

Every inch the movie queen, she tentatively descended the staircase into a lobby of exploding flashbulbs, graciously acknowledging the horde of reporters, still photographers, and cameramen who came to pay homage. They were her court and she had reigned majestically over them for almost fifty years. It was a glorious reminder of the past, when such tributes were commonplace.

William Hurt, who had flown in especially for the occasion, presented the award. I couldn't help but smile. She thought him to be one magnificent hunk.

I'm glad she had that one grand finale. She deserved it.

～ 4 ～

The Ivory Tower

*L*ana returned home to Century City in October 1994 invigorated by the wonderful reception she received in Spain. She enthusiastically set about to prepare for the interview portion of her "Runaway with the Rich and Famous" segment, scheduled to be taped in April 1995.

I realize now that Lana's sudden burst of activity had much to do with her being in remission from her cancer. Friends close to Cheryl tell me her daughter persuaded her to undergo chemotherapy. A year earlier Lana had told me quite emphatically, "I will never let them inject those chemicals into my body." She had a great fear of losing her hair. Her change of mind had no doubt extended her life and enhanced its quality.

Any visit to a medical facility by a movie star alerts the tabloid press, which has spies throughout the medical and legal professions and pays well for information. Lana was a sitting duck. For years the media had been picking up information on her medical problems—sub rosa, of course.

When she was younger, they trailed her, snooping around for any illegal abortions and, later, for evidence of facelifts. Her every trip to Mexico sent up the red flag of "abortion." During Lana's childbearing years abortion was illegal in the United States, so movie stars were spirited quietly across the border to private clinics, on studio payrolls, where unwanted fetuses were quietly removed from their famous wombs.

The tabloid press of the nineties is a highly sophisticated operation. Those who covered Hollywood over the years were quick to pick up, just as I did, Lana's frailty at San Sebastian. A macabre curiosity emerged over her failing health. Was the midnight hour nearing? Would her crystal carriage become a pumpkin? The momentary rush of publicity seemed to be souring.

Upon her return from Spain, she disembarked the plane in a wheelchair, obviously sick and ailing. The clicking and flashing vultures hovered, waiting to move in. When she had been healthy nobody paid any attention to her wheelchairs, which she always requested when we were traveling. She didn't like to walk unless she had to.

She knew what to expect—a negative reaction. She hated being photographed without preparation. Anger turned into outrage when a New York newspaper erroneously reported her death.

In March 1995 she was readmitted to Cedars-Sinai for emergency radiation treatments. The media, expecting her imminent demise, ran unflattering photos of her recent wheelchair experiences. Videos were televised on tabloid programs while the *National Enquirer* ran lurid picture spreads. The vultures were indeed hovering.

She'd been home about three weeks when Robin Leach's crew arrived to do her on-camera interview, which would be interspersed with footage from the film festival. Robin, knowing her precarious health situation, made every effort to accommodate her and arranged for the taping to be done at the Bel Air Hotel.

Her scratchy voice, brought on by her illness and radiation treatments, made it difficult for her to respond to Robin's questions, but Lana, feisty as ever, expressed herself with vigor and determination. She avoided health questions, shifting the interview toward other issues, including her philosophy of living and God, whom she now referred to as her "Power Partner." I like to believe that my sister, Harriet, who would often come over to do Lana's nails, and I had something to do with her new persuasion since we had spoken about religion quite often with Lana.

There was a humorous but somewhat sad aside to all of this. When the interview was broadcast, one piece of footage showed her inside a lovely Spanish church. In a dramatic, hopefully sincere gesture of faith, she'd permitted herself to be photographed praying and making the Sign of the Cross. It never occurred to Lana that she wasn't Catholic. She'd probably repeated this scene numerous times in one of her high-drama soap opera films.

My only thought: *I guess wonders truly will never cease.*

*K*nowing her mother's condition to be terminal, if not critical, it shocked me that Cheryl did not travel as her mother's companion to San Sebastian. I must be an incurable romantic. The only ''family member'' with Lana when she departed this life in the bedroom of her Ivory Tower was her maid and devoted friend of forty-three years, whom Lana referred to as ''my darling Carmencita.''

Carmen related Lana's passing to me on the telephone. Lana had been in her bedroom watching television, as always. From the kitchen Carmen heard Lana calling her name weakly and quickly rushed to her mistress's side.

''What is it?'' she said.

Her response was weak and faint. ''I don't feel well.''

''What is wrong?'' Carmen asked, concerned. Lana did not respond. Only one eye remained open. The color was gone from her once-classic face.

''Lanita, what is wrong?'' Carmen made the sign of the cross as she repeated her question several

times. She reached down and touched Lana's fore-head. Lana took a very deep breath and her head slumped, both eyes now closed for eternity.

Carmen held Lana in her arms. "Lanita," she kept repeating, tears of anguish now flowing freely, but she would never hear another sweet word from the tiny figure she held, like a mother, to her breast.

"But, Carmencita," I interrupted, "wasn't Cheryl there with her mother, like the papers said? Who took care of things?"

"No. Cheryl not here. Me, I did."

I thanked God in my heart that she did not die alone. Knowing Lana's fierce determination to pro-tect her privacy and vanity, Carmen hesitated before calling for help. Then she dialed building security. The security officer responded quickly and sum-moned the paramedics.

Cheryl, who lived but three miles from her moth-er's penthouse, was then notified. When medical help arrived some ten minutes later, Lana Turner was officially pronounced dead.

5

The Beginning

1971–1972

"You look like my father," Lana said, shortly after we'd been introduced. "You remind me of him."

When we first met I had an exclusive contract with the Glenby Corporation, the company that operated the chain of I. Magnin Department Store beauty salons. As style director for the entire Midwest region, I enjoyed an early rush of success. The day I met her, a feature article about me had appeared in the *Chicago Tribune*. My phones hadn't stopped ringing; people were calling to either congratulate me or arrange for appointments.

By nightfall I found myself with a local socialite on my arm, making the rounds, dropping in at various parties. The publicist for Glenby secured invitations for me to attend the most elegant social functions in Chicago. It was considered good for business. Of course, I loved it.

Our last stop of the evening turned out to be the closing night party for *40 Carats*, a play in which Lana had played the lead. We were driven in the company limo to a beautiful townhouse overlooking Lake Shore Drive. Walking through the entry, I scanned the crowd—an interesting mix of social register and theatrical types. Seventy-five or eighty guests were milling about, most of whom I didn't know.

Shortly after our arrival, a dark-haired young man approached me and asked, "Are you the Eric Root featured in today's *Tribune* article?"

"Yes, I am. Why do you ask?"

He introduced himself and said, "Follow me, please."

As my date drifted off toward a group of friends, the young man led me through the crowd toward a woman whose head I could only partially see over the shoulders of those in front of us.

She sat as regal as any empress in a high-backed chair, surrounded by men, and seemed to be holding court. I found it to be an intriguing scene.

"Excuse me, excuse me," the young man said (I would soon find out that he was Lana's personal secretary) as he guided me toward her, gently pushing his way through clusters of guests.

I watched as her eyes flashed in our direction. I could see that she was definitely checking me out as we approached. Those eyes, that face . . .

And then, in her presence, I found myself feeling

more than a little weak in the knees, suddenly recognizing the lovely creature before me. I'd been told she would be the guest of honor, but I never dreamed I'd ever meet her. And I hadn't even seen her play, which further embarrassed me.

"Eric Root," the secretary said, motioning toward her, "I would like you to meet Lana Turner."

She wore a beaded, champagne-colored gown and was still in stage makeup, overly vivid but perfectly applied. Every dazzling inch of her radiated "movie star."

"How do you do," she purred, offering her hand. Her firm handshake and subtle smile captivated me completely.

"How do you do," I replied. "This is a great pleasure." My nerves relaxed slightly as I attempted to gather my composure. She had that special ability to cause one to feel at ease, so we were soon engaged in polite conversation. That's when she mentioned the strong resemblance I bore to her father.

"Miss Turner, I'm surprised," I said, trying to summon up as much charm as possible. "One, I'm so happy to meet you like this, and two, I'm flattered that I remind you of your father."

"And I," she smiled warmly, "am pleased that you addressed me by my last name . . . the sign of a true gentleman."

I came to learn, during my years with her, that she put good manners and proper etiquette high on her list of character traits in others, especially at first meetings.

We continued to hold a general conversation for several minutes. Then she changed the subject.

"I noticed your article in the *Tribune*," she said. "You have quite a reputation."

That she knew about the article both stunned and flattered me. From her next few comments, it became clear to me that she actually *had* read it. The story referred to several of the prominent clients I had, including Rose Kennedy and Marjorie Merriweather Post, when I'd been style director and colorist at Sara Frederick's exclusive specialty store in Palm Beach, Florida. It also mentioned members of the Henry Ford family who'd been clients when I directed the Bonwit Teller salon in Detroit.

Lana always seemed more interested in political leaders and captains of industry than in show business celebrities. She enjoyed people who commanded the wealth, power, and respect of the country, considering them the true American royalty.

"I'm impressed with your credits," she continued, smiling slyly. "Too bad you don't live in Los Angeles. I could use a good hairdresser."

"Miss Turner, if I ever move to California, I will most definitely look you up."

"My dear, you won't have to do that. My secretary will give you my private number." And he did.

At the time, Lana, at fifty, had been a star for thirty years. While no longer the public figure she had been at her peak, she still possessed the beauty, glamour, and zest for life for which she had become so justly famous . . . and infamous. She lived, dressed, loved, behaved, and spent like a glamorous movie queen. She could afford the high life, thanks to huge profit participation in her biggest films of the fifties and sixties, particularly *Imitation of Life* and *Madame X*. Although her latter-day foray into television as the star of a pre-"Dynasty" prime-time soap opera, "The Survivors," did not score high in the ratings, she'd been handsomely compensated. Even though the network canceled the series before the end of its first season, Lana's contract had been paid in full.

No longer in demand for feature film leads—and far too vain to accept the many excellent supporting roles offered—Lana did enjoy an occasional guest shot on television variety programs, for instance, "The Carol Burnett Show." She'd only recently made an interesting discovery: The public—her public— still paid big bucks to see Lana Turner in person.

Venturing into live theater, Lana found herself earning as much as $20,000 a week. By doing *40 Carats*, *The Pleasure of His Company*, and later, *Murder Among Friends* on the road, she would generate a lucrative income throughout the seventies. In 1975 she would add a series of in-person tributes to her list of paid appearances.

By September of 1972 I couldn't stand the thought of enduring another Chicago winter. I'd been approached by the company that ran the chic Saks Fifth Avenue Salon in Beverly Hills. They offered to relocate me and give me their top position. The perks included all my moving and transportation costs and a spacious apartment.

I accepted the generous offer and packed my bags. Within weeks of my arrival I'd settled comfortably into my new surroundings and was looking forward to starting a new life in L.A. A month later I called Lana. I hadn't spoken to her since our first meeting a year ago and I wondered whether she'd remember me.

"Eric, of course I remember you," she said. She sounded excited. "How are you? *Where* are you?"

"I'm in Los Angeles," I said.

"Wonderful! Can you come over?" It surprised me that she wanted to see me so soon. After assuring her I'd be there within the hour, I began adjusting the rest of my day's appointments around Lana, a practice that would continue for the next twenty years.

She lived in a beautiful penthouse in the Edgewater Towers, a luxury high-rise located where Sunset Boulevard meets the ocean in Pacific Palisades. It took some time to get there due to heavy afternoon traffic, but the drive couldn't have been more beautiful. *California* was beautiful!

Carmen answered the door. Entering the apartment, I couldn't help noticing something else besides the ocean-fresh breeze from the terrace. Lana's perfume clung to the air like a romantic Polynesian aphrodisiac. One couldn't easily forget the fragrance. I'm still haunted by it.

"It's called *Tuber Rose* by Mary Chess," she said, when I asked her later. "I'm nearly down to the last drop and I can't find it in the stores around here."

"Let me see what I can do," I said.

The following day I contacted the perfume department at Macy's in New York. "Sorry," the department manager said, "but we're temporarily out of stock."

When I gave them Lana's name and "business number" (actually her apartment), things happened. After confirming that my call referred to the "real" Lana Turner, Macy's located their supply. Within a week ten large bottles of *Tuber Rose* were sitting in Lana's boudoir, air-expressed at no charge from the Mary Chess Company.

Lana preferred that no one else, not even her daughter, Cheryl, wear perfume or cologne in her home. She didn't want any other essence commingling with her own. She thought it might "break the spell." The only men's fragrance she ever cared for—in small doses only, mind you—was *Old Spice*, the cologne worn by her great love, Tyrone Power.

She would sometimes meet me at the door and give me the "sniff" test. "What in the hell is that god-awful stuff you have on?" she shrieked at me one afternoon. "Get out of here. You can't stay . . . it's dreadful."

Then she insisted I take a shower. As commanded, I obediently traipsed through her pastel boudoir to her private bath to cleanse myself of the offending odor.

"Give me your clothes," she yelled through the door, "and I'll have Carmen wash and dry them."

I handed her my jeans and shirt. I emerged a few minutes later, wearing a terry cloth robe. She hugged me and said, "That's better. You smell so clean. What was that horrible stuff, anyway?"

"Lana," I said softly, "*that* was *Tuber Rose* by Mary Chess!"

"I don't believe you," she said, sniffing the air.

"I guess the same scent can smell differently on different people, Lana."

She ignored my explanation. "No one wears that around here but *me*. Got it?"

I got it.

During my early visits to Lana's apartment I quickly discovered something else. She desperately needed a *good* hairdresser—and a total makeover. This legendary beauty, with such incredible bone structure and facial features, looked tired and haggard. Her dressing table told the story. It was covered with a Heinz 57 variety of creams, eye makeup remover, and expensive cosmetics, plus the ever-present tumbler of vodka and an ashtray overflowing with stubbed-out cigarette butts. None of these condiments did anything to enhance her looks.

I also perceived a slight crackle and coarseness

creeping into her girlish voice, which told me that years of hard living were beginning to show. Still, I knew I could do a great deal to restore and enhance the lush Lana Turner look her fans adored. I sat down with her to discuss the possibilities.

"What would you suggest?" she asked. I sensed a tinge of doubt in her voice. "Can you give me a new look?"

I knew she had an important Hollywood premiere to attend soon. She told me it would be nice if "I could turn a few heads" when she exited the limousine. A new image might also catch the attention of the Hollywood press and remind the industry that she represented star power at its zenith.

Delicately I began to explain to Lana the changes necessary to bring her hair, now dried out and splitting from years of improper bleaching, back to life. It hung about her face in an unflattering pageboy, drawing attention to her "down lines." Despite her obvious irritation, she listened until I'd completed my presentation.

"I'm going to place myself completely in your hands, Eric. You can do whatever you think best. I trust you—with one caveat." Her only restriction was that, in making over her hair, I incorporate the famous natural wave that flowed to the left side of her face.

"That's my trademark, honey," she said with a twinkle in her eye.

Within a matter of days I'd devised a new hair

style and reduced her previously lengthy, two-step bleaching process to one single procedure. I used a high-lift blond tint to bring her hair back to its original, healthy condition. Lana, ecstatic, gave me a big hug and a kiss. I'd passed the first "beauty" test.

Ready to get on with her new image, she asked, "Now what can you do about my face?"

Choosing my words with a sense of humorous candor, I said, "Lana, when we first started working together you looked like a Picasso in a Kmart frame."

Dead silence! I instantly regretted my remark when I saw the look of horror on her face. Dead silence! It hadn't occurred to me that I didn't know her well enough to make jokes. I intended it to be a compliment, but she took it the wrong way.

"What the hell did you mean by that?" she asked in what I thought might be mock indignation. It wasn't.

"I didn't mean to be insulting, dear," I said, regaining my footing, "it's just that we've already done great things. Now it's time to finish the job."

She calmed down.

"Honey," she said, with no small amount of suspicion in her voice, "I know you're an artist with hair, but what do you know about makeup?"

"Lana, you know my background in makeup, my work with Revlon and Andre de Paul's Salon in New York." That was where I'd done such notable faces as that of the international modeling sensation, Verushka.

"All right. All right," she said, shrugging. "What *would* you do with my face?"

"Get rid of those *black* eyebrows." She no longer had any natural eyebrows. They'd been shaved in 1938 to create the look of a Eurasian girl in the Gary Cooper film *The Adventures of Marco Polo*. They never grew back and had to be penciled in for the rest of her life.

"Black eyebrows emphasize my eyes."

"They make you look *hard*," I insisted.

Her face froze in defiance. "I will *not* change my eyebrows!" she declared.

She adhered to my other suggestions, particularly my advice to use a lip liner. She also liked the way I applied her rouge, which I did in a manner designed to give her a more suntanned look.

She phoned me the day before the premiere.

"Please forgive me for not inviting you, darling. I don't know what I must have been thinking. But I would like you to join us. I'd like there to be two good-looking blonds in my party," she said sweetly. She couldn't resist adding, "Of course, that's if I like the way my new hairstyle and makeup come together tomorrow night."

"*I* love my new look. It's fantastic," she exclaimed as she took stock of herself in the hall mirror. "You've changed my whole appearance. Thank you, darling."

Then she added the words I'd been waiting to hear. "By the way, I *love* my new eyebrows."

I noticed them the moment I walked in but deliberately refrained from saying anything. They were now a lighter and infinitely more flattering shade of taupe.

That evening heads did turn as all eyes focused on Lana when we walked to our seats in the packed theater. The successful evening heralded a personal triumph for Lana and confirmed my public welcome into her inner circle.

A few nights later I accompanied Lana to a gala fund raiser for Phoenix House, a respected New York drug rehabilitation program. The event took place at Manhattan's famous *Roseland* dance hall. The theme, "A Tribute to the 1940s," brought out most of the superstars from that era. That night I noticed that Lana's demeanor had become more the movie star and less the suspicious, aging actress. It pleased me immensely. I became aware, also, that I didn't get invited to these functions simply because of my charm or suitability as an escort. As a player on Lana's team, my services were indispensable; I had the responsibility of making her look as ravishing as possible.

Uncertain glory accompanied the job, but Lana saw to it that those of us who took care of her caught some of the glow from her spotlight. While not particularly given to compliments in private, she never failed to credit me in public. If someone admired the way she looked, she would quickly point to me and say, "He did it."

I spent hours with Lana in hotel suites, working on her hair and makeup until both were absolute perfection, always with a little twist here and there to create another "new look" for m'lady. That's the way it went for the *Roseland* affair. Thousands of people packed the ballroom to see Bette Davis, Lena Horne, Jane Russell, Alexis Smith, and dozens of others, none of them brighter or more sought after than Lana Turner. Lana, as usual, made a spectacular late entrance, outdazzling her contemporaries and walking away with the evening.

Gradually I came to assume a larger role in her personal life. House calls became something more than just professional visits. We were getting to know each other and developing a deep friendship. After finishing up her hair, we'd often sit around talking and watching television. If an escort failed to show or if she was in the mood for a change, I took her out. She relaxed with me and some of the icy movie queen veneer peeled away. Some, but not all.

In the months and years to follow, I would come to know aspects of Lana's personality few people, even within her own family, ever dreamed existed. I would be with her through highs and lows of incredible magnitude, often becoming the recipient of her love and concern as well as her wrath. On at least one occasion, I would save her life.

I would also come to know the unholy secret haunting her to the end of her days.

◦✂ 6 ✂◦

On the Town

MID-1970s

*A*fter a visit back to Chicago in the mid-1970s, I received a generous offer to return to Florida to become style director once again for the fashionable Sara Frederick's salon in Palm Beach. My clients would be the crème de la crème of Palm Beach society and politics. (Newspaper articles always referred to me as "Eric Root—first, last, and always the society hairdresser.")

Lana asked me not to go, but the professional opportunity was too good to pass up. "Is there anyone in Palm Beach more important than me?" she said.

"Yes, there is, Lana," I said matter-of-factly. I anticipated her reluctance, but I'd made up my mind.

"Who?" she demanded, playing the offended actress.

"Rose Kennedy," I replied.

On the day I was leaving, despite her petulance and pouting, we were both near tears. She wished me good luck. We hugged each other good-bye and promised to talk on the phone every day.

During my absence Lana went to London to make a mediocre picture, *Persecution*, a psychological horror film that turned out to be an imitation of something done better by Bette Davis and Joan Crawford ten years earlier. The picture bombed in Europe and had only a limited release in the United States. Most people never heard of it. Despite her sporadic successes in dinner theaters around the country, where she received hefty salaries (movie stars continue to be big draws in that arena), her film career floundered.

After returning from England, she found a bright light when publicist John Springer put together a tribute in her honor at New York City's Town Hall, celebrating Lana as one of the "Legendary Ladies of the Screen." The evening had been declared a huge success, but I saw the still shots from the event and thought Lana looked like hell. Slightly overweight, her face puffy and bloated, she'd obviously been belting too many double vodkas.

Concerned, I called her the minute she returned to her Ivory Tower. "How come?" I asked.

"Because you've abandoned me, Eric!"

"I would never abandon my spiritual sister," I said. "Besides, I'm tired of Florida. I miss California—and you."

She could barely disguise her pleasure. "Then get

your ass back here!" she chided. "I need you. And darling, it would be so good to see you."

"Really?" I said, inducing her to compliment me in a way she normally didn't.

"Honey, nobody makes me feel better—"

"You're sweet."

"—or makes me look better than you do. And I think," she said, becoming serious, "there's a very special reason for that. You understand what's in my heart. You know my soul."

Whether she was being sincere or not, she touched me. After almost two years, I'd soon be back in California and once again under Lana's spell.

Back in the fold, I opened my own salon in Beverly Hills and resumed my life with Lana as though there'd never been an intermission. Twice a week I did her hair at her home and resumed doubling as her companion at social functions. She'd picked up some bad habits and had been drinking far too much. I reminded her that "goddamn" and "bitch" should be removed from her vocabulary because I found both words offensive. She apologized and promised to make an effort to refrain from their use.

"It's really all your fault," she told me. "I let myself fall back into old habits when you ran away and left me alone."

We enjoyed being back together and she felt more secure in having me there. I particularly noticed that she expressed more affection toward me now than she had in the past. But we had our work cut out for us. The first thing I did was eliminate the hideous pageboy coiffure someone had once again bestowed upon her crowning glory. I also toned down those black eyebrows, which had mysteriously returned, and began to restore her to the more elegant look we'd previously created.

"You need me around to update you," I said, gently touching her shoulder as I restyled her blond tresses into a sophisticated upsweep.

She reached up and patted my hand. "I need you around for more than just updating, darling."

I smiled. "What do you mean, dear?"

"I mean, my darling brother, that I need you in my life."

Our hands clasped to affirm both our feelings. I understood. I'd come home. I needed her, too.

Prior to our first evenings out after my return from Florida, we would sit together in her living room and discuss handling the crowds, the press, and fans. We'd grown so accustomed to each other before I went to Palm Beach that none of these preparations ever seemed necessary. Now I sensed something different in her demeanor. She seemed to develop an unusually bad case of nerves as time grew near for our departure to some social affair. She needed to be constantly reassured that she was still glamorous, sophisticated, beautiful, and, more importantly, *Lana Turner*, an original without peer. I gave her that reassurance.

Not only did she show concern for herself, she'd also decided to coach me, too. "Stand up straight, look strong and friendly, and whatever you do, just act calm," she'd say.

On one particular occasion we were on our way to a premiere and I prayed my nervousness did not show. My nervousness had nothing to do with myself; I was nervous because of Lana. I believed her concern for my demeanor had more to do with her own insecurities. I just wanted to help her make it through the evening, so I said, "Lana, I'm not the calm type, especially in situations like this."

"Well, then, what will make you calm? Do you want a tranquilizer or something?"

I shook my head. "You know I don't take any kind of pills except vitamins."

"But you do enjoy a glass of wine."

Smiling, I reminded her, "Correction. I enjoy a glass of *champagne*."

"Then have a little glass of champagne in the limo on the way."

I'd managed to diffuse her nervousness by permitting myself to become the subject of concern.

And so began a procedure we followed whenever we were chauffeured to any event. Lana would put the final okay to her makeup and I'd sip a glass of champagne, get my "buzz," and our personalities would bloom as we exited the limousine to the roar of the crowd and flashbulbs.

Lana, a great believer in symmetry and color

coordination, had another rather unusual quirk. She was obsessed with appearance, and whenever we were going out she always asked me what I was going to wear. At first I found that odd coming from one so concerned with herself. But I'd tell her, and then she would dress accordingly to complement my suit or blazer, selecting from her fabulous wardrobe gowns, furs, and jewelry that blended with my attire.

In all my days and nights of escorting beautiful women, only Lana showed such consideration. Whatever she selected to wear made me look better. Women could learn a lot from Lana's ability to make a man feel important in public.

She could also be thoughtful and protective in other ways. Aware that I'd been married and fathered a daughter in my early twenties—a daughter I'd not seen in many years—she never probed into my past or made any effort to inquire about my daughter unless I brought up the subject. In due time, of course, I shared everything with her. She passed no personal judgments but showed surprising understanding and compassion.

Our relationship was platonic, but Lana enjoyed the fact that our "dates" raised eyebrows. The tabloids reminded their readers that I was many years her junior and made insinuations about her public appearances with "a man young enough to be her son." Lana just laughed off these comments. Early in her career she'd laid down an ironclad rule: Never be seen in public with a younger man. Now she scoffed at such nonsense. She knew and I knew the truth. We were good friends who enjoyed each other's company, had something better than sex to offer, and loved each other as spiritual brother and sister. Our bonding transcended physical desires.

What the wags and gossips did not know was that Lana and I had each taken a vow of celibacy.

The occasions on which we literally ran across parking lots to escape in-your-face photographers are too numerous to recount. What pictures they managed to get usually appeared in the tabloid press above captions reading "Lana Turner and Her Young Male Companion."

"Fuck'em," she'd mutter breathlessly as we scurried into the security of a limousine. I doubt any journalist could have made out her words, but I did. It became part of a game we played with the media, one that was funny in the beginning, but as the insinuations became more blatant, Lana's anger became difficult to control.

When the *National Enquirer* referred to me as "a gigolo," things had gone too far. My hurt and anger could not be compared to Lana's indignation. The *Enquirer* ran a photo of Lana and me seated at a nightclub table. I, in defiance of Lana's cardinal rule, had been caught with a drink in my hand. The caption made a point of indicating the diamond pinky ring on my little finger, with the innuendo "less than masculine." Lana went through the roof.

"How *dare* they!" she almost shouted, an expression she used when pushed beyond the limits of her endurance. "Who in the hell gave them the right to make such insinuations?"

Her ranting and raving about the *Enquirer* article continued for several days. At first she thought I should sue them for defamation of character, but she changed her mind when I reminded her the publicity would be all about "Lana Turner," with a possible mention of "Eric who?" She never forgave them. I couldn't have cared less.

I think she was most upset about the ring reference. The diamond pinky ring had been her gift.

More and more Lana's chronic lateness to events became an issue not only to her hosts but also between the two of us. I felt that perhaps people thought it was my fault she turned down events or showed up late—or just sent me to give her regrets. I know that makes no sense now, but at the time it concerned me.

This notorious habit had much to do with the undoing of her social and professional standing in a community where social functions result in mega-money movie deals. In Hollywood time and money are the bargaining chips; stories of her late arrivals on the set or at theatrical performances damaged her professional reputation. Eventually, people were more surprised when Lana actually *showed up* than when she didn't.

Vanity—a beautiful woman's snake pit—was the culprit. Increased insecurity about her face became the bane of her existence. If she didn't believe she looked the best possible, she would close the door to the outside world and crawl back into the recesses of her troubled inner self. She'd refuse to leave the Ivory Tower. Even when she thought she looked fabulous, she would still be hesitant, and procrastination would lead to a late arrival. Those seeking reasons to fault her blamed her tardiness on a selfish desire to make an entrance. I knew otherwise.

There would be times when she would emerge from her bedroom, having made numerous changes of gowns and gems, a vision from some heavenly dream. My apprehensions disappeared and we'd be off to a wonderful evening where Lana would outshine any woman who had the nerve to be photographed next to her.

I don't think Lana ever recovered from her association with the death of Johnny Stompanato. She always believed that "one day his Chicago friends will come after me." We might be dining out or enjoying an evening nightclubbing when, without any warning, Lana would grab my wrist and squeeze it tightly. Her face would become pale and I'd see stark terror in her eyes.

"What is it, Lana?"

"Don't look now, but two tables behind you there's some Mafia guys."

"Are you sure?"

"Yes. I know the type. I think they're after me."

"Lana," I'd try to assure her, "there's no reason anybody would want to harm you."

"Yes, there is. They're staring at me. Let's get out of here."

I'd known fear and I recognized it in Lana, so we'd excuse ourselves as politely as possible and with feigned poise and calm we'd quickly exit the scene. Whether or not these "Mafia types" were interested in Lana for any other reason than her celebrity and beauty is unknown to me, but the idea of such a threat became a real source of paranoia in Lana's life.

On numerous occasions, almost always after she'd been drinking, Lana would caution me to be careful. "I don't want anything to happen to you because of me," she'd say.

I believe Lana knew she was safe and secure with me. She knew I wanted nothing from her except her friendship. I served as a buffer, fending off the predatory males who stalk rich and famous ladies. Lana seemed an easy target to that type of man. After all, she'd succumbed to seven marriages, all of which failed, plus the dozens of costly affairs.

Lana and I spent much of the next fourteen years traveling together, having fun and seeing the world through theater tours, book tours, tributes, film festivals, and so forth. Some were spectacular sojourns to Europe and Africa, especially our triumphant visit to Cairo, Egypt, in 1984. I'll always be grateful that knowing Lana Turner led me into vistas that had been mere daydreams to this kid from Michigan. Considering my humble beginnings, I thought at the time that I'd come as far as one possibly could.

Maybe!

✻ 7 ✻

The Legend Hits
the Road

1976

*D*espite the advent of rock 'n' roll, the public has welcomed the occasional resurgence of big-band music. Similarly, the great ladies of the silver screen, unhappy with the girl-next-door syndrome brought on by Doris Day, always expected the public to one day embrace the return of elegance to films. It didn't happen.

Lana did her best to contribute to a "reconstruction" of Hollywood's sophisticated ladies. During the late seventies she kept me busy with her involvement in a variety of projects, all of which were designed to rejuvenate her screen career. She continued touring from time to time with theatrical productions, but motion pictures remained her true calling. She made two films, *Bittersweet Love* in 1976 and *Witches' Brew* in 1978, both of which were big disappointments. Neither was worthy of her talents. I received on-screen credit as her personal hairdresser, and that I found most pleasing.

A serious problem developed in that what few offers Lana did receive involved low budgets. The producers could not afford the star treatment Lana had become accustomed to and demanded. She worried about being "over fifty," as did some of the producers. I totally disagreed. Some of our most popular actresses and performers today are over fifty: Elizabeth Taylor, Vanessa Redgrave, and Carol Burnett come to mind.

Lana, frustrated, openly blamed the industry, her agents, the country's obsession with youth (nothing new about that), everything except the real problem: her own rigid demands. She wanted glamorous roles in *women's* pictures, a category rarely considered profitable in the new era of films. Had she been willing to accept roles designed for the more "mature" woman, there would have been plenty of work. It would be another five years before *television*, surprisingly, resurrected the strong woman in the popular "Dynasty" and "Falcon Crest" TV series.

Lana's life resembled that of a former First Lady, playing the convention circuit for big bucks, mostly to walk out and accept the applause, say a few words, collect her check, and move on to the next convention. The media now referred to Lana as a "legend." Legend kept her occupied. She occasionally appeared in stage productions and on television talk shows—both here and abroad—and became the "nominee" for an increasing number of special honors and awards.

One such event took place during a memorable trip we made to New York City. Blackglama Furs wanted Lana photographed wearing a coat of her choice from their elegant selection. They'd initiated a series of ads titled, "What Becomes a Legend Most?" The chic campaign thrilled Lana and fit her persona exactly. The photographs would appear in only the classiest of fashion magazines worldwide. She would be joining a who's who of legendary predecessors that included Marlene Dietrich, Bette Davis, Joan Crawford, and Claudette Colbert.

On the day of the photo shoot I did her hair and assisted with her makeup. While lighting experts and photographers buzzed over the scene, Lana basked in the glow of the attention being lavished upon her. She would be modeling a gorgeous sable coat she had personally selected from a variety of furs sent over for her approval. The Blackglama people gave her the coat when the session concluded. They had paid all the expenses for our New York stay, and Lana had taken full advantage of their generosity.

Of the several musicals running on Broadway at the time, Lana most wanted to see *Evita*. I knew little of Eva Peron except that she'd been a peasant girl who'd risen to power as the wife of Argentina's dictator, Juan Peron, and succeeded him after his death.

Lana was clearly fascinated by the classic rags-to-riches story. In fact, she herself had a little-known connection to the real Evita Peron, as I would soon find out.

Our limousine approached the theater, where dozens of photographers and fans waited on the sidewalk.

"Who in the hell notified the paparazzi?" she asked.

"I don't know, Lana. Do you want to leave?" I had no idea what to expect.

But her mood was upbeat. "Darling," she said, practicing her exit smile, "it doesn't matter. We look *fabulous* and we're going to have a fantastic evening!"

Relieved, I finished my half glass of champagne. There were times when I underestimated the magnitude of Lana's enduring luminary power. I actually thought the press had amassed for someone else. Lana's years of experience had taught her how these things worked. The theater management, only too happy to provide us with complimentary seats, obviously expected something in return. *They* had notified the press. The end result: a nice set of publicity photographs promoting the play—with a full set, of course, for Lana.

"Honey," Lana said, putting a hand on my arm, "you don't get anything for nothing in this business. Everything's a trade-off." Then she tossed her head back, and with a radiant smile stepped out of the limo into a lightning storm of flashing cameras, dazzling both press and fans. Lana Turner knew how to humble her subjects.

We both loved *Evita* and went backstage afterward to congratulate its dynamic star, Patti LuPone, who was thrilled to meet Lana and suggested we join her for a late supper. Over drinks and a light meal, we were soon chatting like old friends when Lana related an experience she'd had with the real Eva Peron many years ago.

In the 1940s, as one of the world's most beautiful blonds, Lana's films and publicity photographs were widely circulated throughout the Latin countries. South Americans adored her. During her reign as First Lady of Argentina, Evita Peron patterned herself after Lana. In particular, she copied Lana's hairstyles, makeup, and tailored suits, which Lana popularized on the screen.

Lana had occasion to meet Evita Peron briefly at a party when she toured South America in 1946. She described the meeting as brief, eerie, and uncomfortable. She felt as if she'd been microscopically scrutinized by Madame Peron. And indeed, she had.

Lana had a kicker to her story. Sometime after she'd returned to MGM from Argentina, the MGM hairdressing department received a panicky phone call from Madame Peron's secretary. Argentina's First Lady had instructed her personal hairdresser to bleach her hair the same shade of blond as Lana Turner's. He botched the job. Evita's hair became a

bright *orange*, just days before she would be address-
ing an important political assembly.

In the interest of international diplomacy—
and not in the least, a lucrative South American
market—MGM came to the rescue, instructing Helen
Young, Lana's personal hairdresser at the studio, to
wire her secret hair color formula to Eva Peron. She
included one important stipulation: Lana's natural
auburn hair was much lighter than Eva's black
tresses, so the amount of bleach would need to be
increased. Presumably it worked. Evita, throughout
her political career, continued to sport her Lana
Turner look until her early death at age thirty-three.

Patti LuPone listened intently, excited at gaining
these new insights into the background of the famous character she portrayed nightly.

Bad news awaited our return to Los Angeles,
however. Lana's late curtain calls and no-shows had
caught up with her. The dinner theater people were
losing interest. Producers, leery of paying the large
advance guarantees she demanded, didn't want to
take a chance on her anymore. In the face of dimin-
ishing returns, another method for augmenting
Lana's income would have to be found. Fate presented a new opportunity.

Following her enormously successful 1975 tribute as one of the "Legendary Ladies of the Screen" at
New York City's Town Hall, Lana was offered a kind
of traveling version of the same event. She liked the
idea. Not only would the appearances keep her name

before the public in a positive manner, but the continuous press attention would also nurture the movie star myth and Lana's unfailing sense of self-importance.

Only the most prestigious theaters in major cities were scheduled. San Francisco attorney Melvin Belli's wife, Lia, would be using her considerable contacts and influence to assure a successful tour.

The simple tribute format rarely varied. After screening a montage of stunning film clips from her film career, Lana would walk out on stage to a thunderous standing ovation, trade quips with the host, and answer questions from the audience (preselected to prevent any embarrassing inquiries about Johnny Stompanato).

Based loosely on publicist John Springer's popular "An Evening With . . ." celebrity programs, the concept caught on and soon other "legends" followed suit: Cary Grant and Bette Davis began appearing on stages in other cities. The idea eventually spread to college campuses and cruise ships and continues today as a lucrative enterprise.

Lana was remunerated handsomely for her appearances and provided all the trappings befitting a Hollywood movie queen. To avoid the suggestion of any improprieties or greed, a small, well-publicized portion of the profits from these engagements was donated to the star's favorite charity. Lana's contribution was to go to "Bean Sprouts," a series of television programs designed to promote aid and understanding for Chinese-American children. Unfortunately, "Sprouts" ultimately did not benefit much from Lana's tour because of her constant tardiness and failure to attend press conferences to promote her appearances. The audiences at her tributes began getting smaller, and as her in-person draw diminished, so did box office receipts.

Following a poorly attended appearance in New Orleans, we limped into Miami Beach and checked into the Frank Sinatra Suite at the Fontainebleau Hilton Resort and Towers. Frank and Lana were old (some say intimate) friends, and she wouldn't hear of staying anywhere else.

Befitting the Chairman of the Board himself, the Sinatra Suite, a two-story residence on the hotel's sixteenth and seventeenth floors (occupied by Ol' Blue Eyes whenever he visited Miami), featured a dramatic white marble entry that opened onto an enormous living room with huge picture windows overlooking a sizable portion of the Atlantic Ocean and Miami Beach. The main floor featured a well-stocked bar, a billiards room with big-screen TV, and a complete kitchen with a formal dining room. Black marble stairs led to a second-floor arrangement of three bedrooms with adjoining baths. In this state of mind and rarefied atmosphere all hell would soon break loose.

❈ 8 ❈

Moon Over Miami,
Blood in the Frank
Sinatra Suite

WINTER 1976

"**I**'m gonna *kill* that bitch!"

The man stood by the shattered window, directing his angry words at Lana, who was cowering with fear in her room at the other end of the hall.

Seventeen floors below us Miami Beach glittered. In the Frank Sinatra Suite vodka flowed freely. Lana and this man played an increasingly dangerous game of cat and mouse, each goading and taunting the other into a high-rise game of chicken.

As the only sober person present (watching the tension mount between these two for half an hour), I faced a tortured individual who threatened to kill our famous employer.

What had begun as an exciting personal appearance tour for Lana had suddenly degenerated into a nightmare.

Lana's increasingly volatile relationship with her male secretary had reached its end. After years of trying to guide his legendary but undependable star through a series of failed film projects, aborted personal appearances, and late theater curtains, he'd reached the end of his patience. Unfortunately, both Lana and he were heavy drinkers with a decided flair for the dramatic. It did not help that the secretary had a history of epileptic seizures for which he took medication, a dangerous combination with alcohol.

We returned to the suite from a reasonably well attended Lana Turner tribute. Sparkling lights along the shoreline disappeared into the blackened horizon. Lana, in a good mood and still high from the evening, floated toward the bar.

"Look at that moon," I said as we poured ourselves a nightcap; champagne for me, vodka for Lana and her secretary.

"Moon over Miami," Lana said, toasting the perfect cliché for the moment. She knew how much I loved Miami.

We were chatting about the evening when we noticed that the secretary seemed to be brooding and becoming more morose by the minute. I sat down to discuss the next day's itinerary with him when he abruptly announced he would be needing several days off. He seemed distraught as he explained to Lana that his daughter had run away from the home of his former wife in Los Angeles, and he must find her. To do so meant leaving the tour and returning to California.

"But you can't go. You wouldn't even know where to start looking," said Lana, concerned for his daughter, but more than a little alarmed at the thought of losing her right-hand man.

"You should definitely stay here with me," she continued firmly. "I'm sure her mother is doing everything she can. There's nothing you can do there. I need you . . . right here . . . right now!" Lana's insistence triggered an explosive mechanism, setting the secretary off on a path from which there would be no return.

She had meant, of course, that she depended on him to help her finish the tour. All too often Lana's reasoning came out sounding calculated and selfish. Had she really expected him to put his allegiance to her above his allegiance to his own flesh and blood? I caught the wild look in his eyes and knew she'd pushed him too far.

After slugging down his fourth or fifth drink in rapid succession, he stood, gave us both a demented go-to-hell look, and staggered up the curving marble stairway leading to the second floor.

A few seconds later we heard the delayed explosion. Suddenly, a blood-curdling animalistic noise came from the upper level; guttural howling and wailing beyond comprehension. We were treated to the sounds of doors slamming and furniture being knocked about, accompanied by insults to Lana and myself, followed by the announcement that he intended to kill himself. I thought the entire hotel must be hearing his tirade.

Lana's first reaction? She was startled but skeptical, as if she thought he was merely staging a scene or throwing a tantrum to get attention. Then I saw the fear in her eyes. Something had gone seriously wrong. Afraid not to take his talk of suicide seriously, I went upstairs to take inventory. Lana followed, hurrying past me to her own room at the opposite end of the hall.

Using some questions about our future plans as a pretense, I cautiously entered his room. He stood by the bedroom window, his back to me and the doorway.

"That fucking bitch doesn't give a shit about anyone but herself!" he said, picking up a large glass ashtray from the nightstand by his bed. Suddenly he flung the ashtray *through* the plate glass window. The sound of shattering glass pierced the night. Voices shouted out from other rooms to "hold it down."

"I'm gonna *kill* that bitch!" he screamed.

"What are you doing? Stop it! Get hold of yourself!" I said. I had no idea what he might do next. Then, just as quickly, his mood changed.

"I really do feel like jumping," he said solemnly. He tottered beside the half-empty windowsill, grasping the shards of broken glass in his bare, bloodied hands. More blood ran down the wall as he stood there, staring down at the street seventeen floors below. The window, located fairly high on the wall, didn't offer the easiest exit from the room and didn't seem large enough for him to get his body through. Still, in his state of mind I thought he might actually jump. I'd never encountered anything so bizarre.

"Why would you want to kill yourself?" I asked cautiously. "What about your daughter? She needs you." I tried to be calm, to reassure him that everything would be okay if he'd just calm down.

"Because I hate my life. I hate Lana Turner! I hate catering to that bitch!" I could see his rage returning, so I backed slowly out the door and headed down the hall to Lana's bedroom.

"Lana, he's crazy," I said, standing in her doorway.

"Honey, I know. Get inside." She pulled me into the room. "He'll be coming here next. Close the door and lock it," she said, her voice low and nervous.

"Lana, I really don't think . . ."

"You don't know his personality like I do," she said, interrupting. She slammed the door and locked it herself. Almost immediately he knocked on the door, trying the handle. Then he began pounding. Lana *did* know him. It wasn't over yet.

"Lana, let me in," came the voice from outside.

"No," she replied.

"Let me in or I'll put my foot through the fucking door!" The anger in his voice had risen, his words now slurred.

"No!" she yelled.

Then he tried a different ploy. "Lana, please. I just want to talk. Let me in." He spent the next minute or two pleading his case in a softer, more reasonable manner. But Lana stood her ground.

"Lana," I finally said, trying to bring the standoff to an end, "let him in. I'll be here with you, and we can try to talk things over rationally. It's better than causing any further disturbance. Besides, we can't stay in here forever."

She gave me an incredulous look, rolled her eyes as if to say, "All right, but don't say you haven't been warned," and gulped down some more vodka.

I opened the door and he calmly entered the room, almost in slow motion. His eyes were glazed over. Then Lana saw the blood. His cut and bleeding hands dripped blood over the pale, cream-colored carpet.

"Lana, I have to find my daughter," he began in a conciliatory tone of voice, almost pleading.

"I told you, I need you here. Let your wife handle it," she said, refusing to waver from her earlier stance. I could see we were going to be in trouble again.

"I don't give a shit what you need!" he screamed.

"You can't go," she insisted. "Who's going to help me finish the tour and take care of the travel arrangements? I certainly can't be expected to do it."

"Fuck 'em!" he shouted, "And fuck you!"

"But you are *my* employee!" she screamed back, in what seemed like a deliberate challenge.

"Yeah, yeah. I'm your employee, your secretary, your *lover*, your stooge. . . ." His voice trailed off in a series of unintelligible words.

"Lana, be careful," I said in an effort to cool down the confrontation just as he lunged toward her, arms outstretched, hands still dripping blood, reaching for her throat.

"I'm gonna strangle you, bitch!"

I jumped between them, blocked his assault, and shoved him backward. "Get out!" I shouted.

"Fuck you, asshole. You're next!" He rammed into me with surprising strength. However, in his drunkenness his coordination failed and he started staggering in circles. It occurred to me that he might be having a seizure. I dodged as he swung back around toward me, reeled him around, and shoved him out the door. I locked the door behind him, hearing a flat thud as he landed in the hallway. Then the pounding on the door resumed.

"He's not giving up," said a now terrified Lana. She stood a few feet from me, crying and shaking like a leaf. "He intends to kill us!"

On the possibility that she might be right, I grabbed the phone and called hotel security. Within seconds two guards used a passkey to enter the suite (I can only assume they'd already been alerted by complaints from other guests).

Following the trail of blood along the upstairs

hallway, they grabbed the ranting, irrational creature outside Lana's bedroom and attempted to sub-
due him. As he kicked and flailed his arms like a wild
animal, they forcibly removed him from the prem-
ises, his bloodied hands bound in restraints behind
his back.

"Let go of me, you assholes! You can't do this.
I'm her secretary!" he yelled, glaring back at Lana
as the guards dragged him away. His screams and
threats echoed down the hotel corridor.

Lana struggled to compose herself for the all-
important scene she would soon play for the Fontainebleau's night manager, who arrived shortly
after the security men. She would need his sympathy and cooperation in order to defuse a potentially
explosive media circus.

The entire hotel knew there were problems in the
Frank Sinatra Suite. Everyone—the management,
other occupants, bellboys, night maids—knew
something terrible had happened, or nearly happened, on the seventeenth floor. The incident had
been loud, long, and nasty. With the secretary out of
the way, Lana turned to her new problem—*the press.*

In an effort to avoid undesirable publicity, she deliberately had not called the police or pressed
charges. Ever since the Stompanato murder she'd
been frightened of another violent incident in which
she would play a major role. The night manager understood. Instead of having the police take her secretary off to the drunk tank, which would certainly

have alerted the media, the security personnel deposited him in another room at the hotel where he could sleep it off. A house doctor administered a sedative and cleansed his wounds.

The following day, much to Lana's horror, a Miami newspaper carried a brief story about the incident. Fortunately, details were sketchy and, although the item included Lana's name, the entire matter had been reduced to a "disturbance." However, reporters from the tabloids, smelling the scent of blood, began to circle like sharks, approaching me as well as several members of the hotel staff and offered sizable sums of money to anyone willing to discuss the incident. To my knowledge, no one ever did.

Because of the fear of more adverse publicity, Lana did not fire the secretary—*not yet*. She needed him to complete the tour, which included a very important stop in Atlanta. For the next few days her steps would be dogged by persistent reporters, still trying to dig into the Miami incident. Whenever cornered, Lana deflected questions skillfully.

Atlanta, our final stop, was the last straw. Fortified with vodka and prescription drugs, the secretary remained moody and belligerent. Lana asked him to stop drinking, making no reference whatsoever to her own problems with alcohol. Once again she pushed the wrong button. He blew up. This time he became physically abusive, pushing her down onto the floor. Lana shoved her knee into his groin, got up from the floor, and ran into her bedroom. She locked the door, then telephoned my room. I got there as fast as I could, bringing with me Lia Belli and Phil Sinclair, the tour producer.

In our presence Lana demanded the secretary return her credit cards, airline tickets, and the key to her house. His embarrassment and anger at being dressed down in front of us was all too obvious. I expected the worst.

Instead, he reached into his briefcase and produced several envelopes and a ring of keys. Perhaps he'd decided to be reasonable. "Take them, bitch!" He threw the keys at Lana, barely missing her face.

Lia, Phil, and I quickly moved in to surround Lana and held our breaths. We all knew a good exit line when we heard one and hoped the confrontation had run its course, that he would leave quietly and a sigh of relief could be heard from all. Lana's eyes hardened into pure hatred. She'd been threatened for the last time. Worse, she'd been upstaged.

"That's it! Get out. You're fired!" she shouted.

But he had already turned away, walking out of her life forever.

~⚐ 9 ⚐~

The Bad and the Beautiful

*T*o me Lana Turner's single greatest flaw rested on one hard delusion: She believed in her own publicity. That might be said of so many film luminaries. This statement, or variations of it, can be traced back to fan magazine articles of the 1940s. In Lana's circumstance, it became as true in her later years as it had been in her youth.

The woman loved the essence of her manufactured image, crafted and carefully remolded over the years like too many coats of paint on an old house that eventually began to peel away, revealing an aged Dorian Gray visage. This was endlessly reflected in the roles she chose and the plush designer worlds her characters inhabited. It's more than just a coincidence she continued playing wealthy, glamorous women smoldering in melodrama in most of her later films.

For Lana, the artifice had become real. How else

could one explain the years of spoiled self-indulgence at MGM? Her extravagant concepts of beauty and romance? The unceasing rumors of her countless affairs? Ultimately, the plot twists of her most lurid films were matched and often surpassed by incidents in her private life.

By the time I met Lana she had already bought into her personal myth, continuing to live it on a grand scale. Even in semiretirement the queen still revered the monarchy and every glorious word ever written about her. She would go to her grave impressed by her exalted position and the power it could wield.

The attainment of stardom was governed by rules of conduct—two sets of rules, in fact: one for a star's private life and another for public viewing. In the thirties and forties the price of fame came with something called a morals clause, a contract stipulation whereby the studio could dismiss a player for conduct unbecoming. Lana, like other valuable "properties," knew how to play the game and get around anything, usually with the assistance of the studio.

From her earliest days the public saw Lana as an enchanting wind-up doll. This image was created not by accident but through carefully planned programming by MGM. In interviews she appeared alluringly feminine and shy, an appealing mix of sparkle and vulnerability. Any hint of the precocious and worldly young woman rapidly developing just beneath the surface was discouraged, and most likely even forbidden.

A quick study, she gladly allowed herself to be photographed chatting with her fans and signing autographs, especially when the newsreel cameras were rolling. She learned never to be photographed with a cigarette or a drink in her hands. Later, in the forties, Hollywood's glamorous actresses refrained from being seen publicly with a younger male companion or one of unsavory character. Lana maintained that policy until she met Johnny Stompanato in 1957.

Lana spent long hours perfecting new ways to display herself to better advantage. She knew, for instance, which were her best angles, and knew never to permit herself to be photographed at dinner parties in unposed situations. Forty years later, film veterans would tell me, "Ah, but she has always been so sharp. She knows this business inside out."

She quickly learned that she looked best in fitted, tailored suits and expert makeup that made her look fresh and natural. Whenever possible, she relied on the considerable resources of the studio to dress and make her up for personal and public appearances. The end result? A flawless apparition, perfect for public consumption.

Until the Stompanato murder, Lana enjoyed a long and reasonably successful relationship with the press. If one of her off-screen affairs or escapades looked as though it was going to soil her image, she knew how to clean up after herself. She'd pick up the phone and call a powerful ally—the Hearst newspaper chain's top gossip queen, Louella Parsons. She could grant an *exclusive* interview to clear up all the "lies and misconceptions." In Hollywood's Golden Age, such tactics worked like a charm. The public wanted gorgeous Lana to be above reproach and with the studio press corps constantly extolling her virtues, that's exactly what they got.

Things change, though. Today the public wants dirt—and they get it.

Privately, Lana Turner smoked like a chimney, drank like a fish, swore like a sailor, and made love with indiscriminate abandon. When I met her she hadn't changed, and was still indulging in most of these habits. I quickly saw the contrast between her ladylike deportment in public and the disregard for convention she often displayed in private.

Lana knew I hated her constant swearing and use of vulgarity. In later years, especially when she'd been drinking heavily, she would slip up, often shocking those within earshot who didn't know her. I beseeched her to tone down the language, especially when it came to uttering the phrase, "Goddamn it!" Later, when we were more spiritually in tune, she made a conscious effort to stop taking the Lord's name in vain, at least in my presence. Other verbal habits weren't so easy to break.

She spouted the "F" word all too frequently, raising eyebrows and cheapening her self-described image as a "lady." Apparently she'd been saying "fuck" since her teens and found it difficult to remove from her vocabulary. It remained, along with "bullshit," "son of a bitch," "bastard," "asshole," and her favorite when denouncing another female, "bitch." No one could upstage her with expletives.

Drinking became a far more serious problem. She often said she could sip one drink all evening, and while that may have been true in the past, I now watched her develop a serious dependency on vodka. It became an insidious and cumulative problem. Alcohol inevitably brought out the worst aspects of her personality.

Sober, Lana was everything her fans could have dreamed—considerate, loving, thoughtful, and *funny.* She could be surprisingly shy and vulnerable, yet she possessed a marvelous sense of humor and an ability to laugh at herself. When I think of her now I honestly believe that to be the true essence of Lana: the youthful, innocent, exuberant Lana Turner under all the furs and jewels, before she ever set foot in Hollywood.

Drunk? That's a different story. Under those circumstances Lana changed into another person altogether—selfish, nasty, sarcastic, manipulative, and totally full of herself. I often wondered if she understood just how self-destructive her behavior had become. When I broached the subject she'd only shrug, as if to say, "So what?" There's no question in my mind she was, and had been for a long time, indulging in guilt-ridden self-punishment and, deep down, I think she knew it.

"Why didn't you shoot her face?" Kirk Douglas, playing a movie producer, asked Barry Sullivan, playing a director, regarding Lana's character in *The Bad and the Beautiful*.

"She was drunk," was Sullivan's sobering reply.

By the mid-1960s Lana found herself in exactly the same situation. Despite a fabulous million-dollar wardrobe, her work on *Love Has Many Faces*, shot on location in Acapulco, was nearly unsalvageable.

Either hung over or sick throughout much of the shooting, she totally absented herself from the set a record number of days. Among other problems, Lana had what is known in the business as a "camera eye," a strained muscle causing her left eye to gradually close from the hot, bright lights on a film set. This meant her close-ups could be filmed only during the first two hours of the morning—that is, if she showed up and was sober.

During production Lana came down with a bad case of Montezuma's revenge. She lost a great deal of weight, which created tremendous continuity problems. It became all but impossible to match the footage filmed earlier. It took several weeks to build up her weight so she could get back to work. To make matters worse, for the first time in her career, Lana's close-ups were filtered to soften the obvious deterioration showing in her face.

Now forty-five, she'd begun to experience serious doubts about her looks, career, and durability as a femme fatale. Acapulco had always been one of her favorite playgrounds. Married or single, she always had fun in Acapulco, and loved staying in the Lana Turner Bungalow at Teddy Stauffer's Villa Vera. In the early 1950s she counted the president of Mexico among her admirers. He gifted her with a dazzling bracelet made of gold, turquoise, and diamonds.

To this day several of my friends who remember Lana's visits to Acapulco insist that on several occasions the beaches were littered with her indiscretions. Beach boys, bartenders, waiters, and hotel guests were said to have been the recipients of her favors. Another friend and client who is still very well connected in Mexico City recalled similar rumors about Lana that circulated in the country's highest political circles.

Lana's alleged behavior came uncomfortably close to the plot of *Love Has Many Faces*, in which she played Kit Jordan, one of the world's wealthiest women, who was drowning herself in alcohol and men along the beaches of the Mexican Riviera.

The stories of Lana's experiences in Mexico were by no means isolated exceptions. For years rumors of her sexual proclivities were already legendary within the Hollywood underground. My friend and noted press agent, the late Rupert Allen, once told me a story he swore to be gospel. During her single days, it seems Lana, who was starring in one of her less demanding potboilers at MGM, decided—or, rather, insisted—that she had to get laid before she could continue with the afternoon's filming. Since hundreds of technicians, actors, and extras would be left standing idle (and on salary), a studio flunky was quickly dispatched to find a stud to service the star.

A short time later, a muscular hunk showed up on the Culver City sound stage and was escorted directly to Lana's dressing room. Rupert laughed when he got to the story's payoff. It seems the stud did his job so well that Lana eventually ended up marrying him! The stud, by the way, was Lex Barker.

Oddly enough, the Jekyll-and-Hyde aspect of Lana's public versus private life was not entirely an act. She truly enjoyed life as a star and genuinely appreciated her admirers, especially her younger masculine fans. Although rocked by a midcareer scandal few stars could have survived, her fans remained loyal. Publicly, at least, she would try not to disappoint them again.

She believed, however, that a small segment of her following had crossed the line and become borderline fanatics. Certain adults, including some members of the press, who spent their time following, photographing, and studying her every move, gave her cause for concern. She'd be outraged if they ran alongside her limousine, tapping on the windows, or tried to hug, kiss, or otherwise touch her in any way. While she may not have minded any of this in her youth, she hated any close contact or gawking as she grew older. She had nothing but contempt for anyone who pursued her in this manner. "Lanatics," she called them.

During the last few years of her life, she became increasingly suspicious of collectors and promoters who traded in Lana memorabilia, which included films, movie posters, signed photos, and fan magazine articles. She felt these people were just like all the other opportunists in Hollywood, making money off her likeness and image. In 1980 she stopped giving autographs altogether, convinced that every time she wrote her name across a poster or photograph she enhanced its value for someone else.

"Why should I sign these things?" she asked me one day when I brought her a poster to inscribe for one of my friends. "So these scavengers can profit? I'm *through* making money for other people."

It saddened me to see Lana growing bitter over such petty issues, but I understood her frustration. I saw misplaced hostility born out of inactivity. Whether she wanted to work or not, there were no offers.

~ 10 ~

The Downhill Slide

1980

"*I* am not going to watch you die!" I said, grabbing Lana by both arms and forcing her to look me in the eyes and listen.

She'd just been diagnosed with a potentially fatal malady. Not even Cheryl knew (I doubt Lana ever told her). Her specialist, being brutally blunt, told her what she must do if she expected any possibility of survival. She shook like a fragile blossom in my arms, barely able to stand up alone, telling me she didn't think she could do it. Her once-gorgeous face had taken on the sunken hollows of a cadaver.

"And furthermore," I insisted, "either you get off the booze, or I'm leaving you!"

"Fine," she screamed, pushing me away. "Then get the hell out of here! Go!"

The harshness of her words cut deeply. Couldn't she see that I cared? Evidently not. I remember thinking as I made my way down the corridor toward the elevator, *Well, if that's how it's going to be, I never want to see her again.* I'd be damned if I just sat by and watched her kill herself. But even as these thoughts raced through my head, I knew our relationship hadn't ended.

As I've often said, my life with Lana never had a dull moment. We weathered the seventies together and, one way or the other, we'd make it through the eighties.

*B*y the end of the 1970s Lana—physically, emotionally, and professionally depleted, her days of live performance on the stage drawing to a close—needed to take serious stock of her life. Her successful regional tours in *40 Carats* and *The Pleasure of His Company* were long over. A revival of *Bell, Book and Candle* had received moderate reviews with audiences to match. Her plans to take on yet another play, *Murder Among Friends* (written especially for her), on tour and then to Broadway were doomed from the start by Lana's reputation for unprofessionalism while touring—and the ever-present consumption of vodka.

The strained relationship between Lana and her daughter grew more distant, literally and symbolically, when Cheryl and Josh moved to Honolulu, followed shortly thereafter by Lana's mother, Mildred. Lana made an effort to keep in touch with her tiny family through frequent trips to Honolulu. In the early eighties she leased an apartment there. I usually didn't accompany her on these trips, partly because they were family visits. Also, I had my salon business to maintain and had recently started giving beauty lectures around the country.

Judging by Lana's despondent or angry moods when she came back from the islands, the visits were not always pleasant encounters. On one occasion she phoned from Los Angeles International Airport, having just arrived on a flight from Honolulu.

"Darling, I've got to tell you something before you see me. I need to prepare you." She had difficulty controlling her emotions.

"What are you talking about? Lana, are you all right?"

"I think so," she stammered. "There are . . . some bruises on my face. I'm a little black and blue."

"What bruises? What happened to you, Lana?" Had she had a bad encounter with some strange man? I couldn't imagine what could have happened.

"I'm okay. Just call it a minor confrontation." Her voice contained a touch of irony.

"Confrontation? With whom?" I asked, my concern growing. There had to be more to this. But Lana, ever the actress, couldn't help but build to a dramatic conclusion.

"With Cheryl," she finally whispered, as though someone might be listening to our conversation. "You know my daughter can be a little rough sometimes. She still holds certain things against me."

As she spoke those words I remembered her many references to Cheryl's "horrible, stubborn nature" and "ability to do me in good."

In her autobiography, *The Legend, the Lady, the Truth*, Lana elaborated on her daughter's rebellious nature, saying, "Her defiance had a tough edge making her impossible to control."

If she sometimes "got rough" as Lana claimed, she could easily overcome her mother. Cheryl had the advantage of being considerably larger than her mother, both in height and weight.

I arrived at Lana's apartment a few hours later. The woman who answered the door had a long, dark bruise along her jawline near the chin. She apologized, adding, "There are bruises on my body that I don't want you to see."

"What the hell did she do to you?" I demanded.

"Everything seemed okay. We'd had dinner, the three of us, and had several drinks afterward. We had a minor argument, Cheryl and I, and then . . ."

Lana neglected to mention who started the ruckus that followed. Apparently mother and daughter began tossing verbal barbs at each other. The verbal abuse, according to Lana, intensified to the point where Cheryl and Lana actually began slapping each other.

"You know, Eric," Lana continued, "what hurt the worst wasn't what she did to me. Josh held me down while Cheryl beat me. *Repeatedly!* That hurt!"

Lana, with dark sunglasses in place and a double

coat of makeup on her bruised face, had sneaked through VIP channels at the Honolulu Airport, un-recognizable behind the glasses and a scarf that covered most of her face. Her story infuriated me. Lana had a tendency to embellish the telling of a story, but she'd always been basically honest with me throughout our relationship. I could think of no reason for her to lie to me now. And she had the bruises to validate her story.

"I'm going to call Cheryl and let her know how I feel about this. Doesn't she know you're not well?" I said in haste.

"No, Eric, leave it alone," she insisted. "Thank you for being concerned, my darling brother, but this is between Cheryl and me. There are some things I must handle in my own way."

Lana had a far more serious situation to face than her personal or professional problems: her rapidly deteriorating health. During her most recent tour with *Murder Among Friends*, she missed countless performances—no longer unusual behavior—and a great deal of money had to be refunded at the box office. Her weight plummeted and her once-glowing face took on an emaciated look. Although she refused to eat, she steadily nursed her vodka both day and night. Her lethargic attitude terrified me. If something didn't change, and quickly, Lana's remaining life could be counted in weeks, not months.

Expecting the worst I insisted she go to a highly recommended holistic specialist, Dr. Jus Want

Khalsa. Getting her to his office posed a major problem. I bundled her up in babushka, scarf, and dark glasses and supported her firmly all the way into the doctor's office.

Dr. Khalsa performed an exhausting series of blood tests. "Miss Turner," he plainly explained, "you are at the beginning stages of *cirrhosis of the liver.*" He added, "If you continue your present habits, your condition will most certainly prove fatal."

A Sikh convert, Dr. Khalsa had been diplomatic with Lana, but most direct. "If you want me to be your physician," he went on, "and if you want me to help you get well, you have to do something for me."

"And what, may I ask, is that?" Lana asked.

"Stop drinking! Immediately!" he commanded, raising his voice.

"How do you know I'm drinking?" she demanded. "And how dare you insult me this way!" Lana's attempt at offense had the effect of a weak defense. Even at death's door she had to be an actress.

Calmly the doctor picked up her file and thumbed through it. "Miss Turner, these are your blood chemistry reports."

Lana's mouth started to quiver, and her eyes moistened. She reached into her purse for a handkerchief, stood up, and tried to regain her composure.

A more subdued Lana spoke, slowly. "I have to leave now, doctor, because I have to deal with this on my own . . . in private. I'll call you tomorrow, after I've had time to think and meditate on the matter. Thank you for your time."

I helped her out of the doctor's office. Although visibly shaken by what the doctor had told her, she said, "I'm not coming back here. What does he know?"

For several weeks she lived in denial. After watching her health continue to fail, I finally had to speak out again.

I confronted her one afternoon. She had been drinking. "Lana, you're so frail and thin. You look like a ghost. Please, you've got to do something!"

"I'll meditate," she said.

I suggested taking it a step further by opening the Bible together, convinced we would find guidance there. But Lana's spiritual philosophy involved seeking answers from within herself.

"I don't need the Bible, darling. I just have to make my own decision as to whether I want to do this or not."

"My God, darling, look in the mirror. If you don't do what the doctor says, *you're going to die*!"

"Eric, don't torture me."

"Then don't do this to me," I responded. "Dammit, I can't stand the way you're treating your life and death situation. You heard the doctor. You have only one way to survive. You've got to cleanse your system of alcohol so he can start your treatment."

She looked so fragile, so weak and vulnerable.

She trembled as I put my arms around her. I held her close to me, to reassure her that everything would be all right if she'd just trust me. I could feel the struggle being waged inside her.

"Oh, Eric, I just don't think I can do it." She looked at me pitifully, hopelessly, her eyes filling with tears.

I took a step back and braced her shoulders so she could see the sincerity in my eyes. "You are not alone, Lana. I am here with you all the way. I am not going to stand by and watch you die!"

"So who asked you to?" she challenged, her voice weaker than intended.

"Darling, you're my sister, my very best friend, and I love you. I can't stand to see your condition worsen or for you to suffer. You wouldn't want to stand by and watch me die, would you?"

"Why do you keep saying that I'm going to die?"

"Look, Lana, Dr. Khalsa gave you a diagnosis and his prognosis. Are you going to accept it or not?"

"How dare you! You've offended me. You're talking to me like a child. You know how hard this is for me." Cupping her chin in her hand, she turned her face away. "You are some kind of friend."

"Excuse me, but maybe you'd better take a look around. It looks like I'm the only friend you've got right now. You think that bottle of vodka is your friend? I'm telling you, Lana, as much as I do care, if you don't get off the booze, I'm leaving you . . . for good!"

She began screaming at me, telling me to get the hell out of her apartment, out of her life. So I started to collect my things. I left her standing in the doorway. By the time I reached the elevator I'd started to cry. The look on her face as I left was one I'd seldom seen before, as though she'd regressed to a small child, desperate for someone to love and protect her through a nightmare. I remember pushing the "down" button and thinking, *If I have to leave her in order to wake her up, then so be it!*

I looked back before entering the elevator which would take me out of her life, and saw her standing in the hallway, tears streaming down her cheeks, her arms open to me. I dropped my bags and rushed back to her. She hugged me with all the remaining strength she possessed, buried her head in my chest, and whispered, "Oh, Eric, I need you. . . . I do need you."

I picked her up and carried her back into her apartment. We sat for hours on the sofa, holding each other, talking, reasoning together. She touched my heart when she said she needed me. I knew I could never really abandon her.

By the time we went to bed, about four in the morning, we'd mapped out plans for her recovery. Her good-night words to me were the best I could hope for: "Eric, I do not want another drink."

The following morning I phoned Dr. Khalsa.

By that early afternoon we were sitting in his

office at Cedars-Sinai Medical Center, listening to him outline details for Lana's treatment and therapy.

"In addition to giving up all alcohol, I'm giving you forty-three different pills to take, Lana . . . all herbs."

"But how will I swallow all of that?" she asked.

"I'll tell you the same thing I tell all my patients. Get a little masher or spoon and crush them together. Then add the powder to juice, cereal, whatever is easiest for you. Just be sure you do it."

For once in her life Lana listened. She followed Dr. Khalsa's instructions religiously, determined to get well as quickly as possible. She now had hope and the belief that she could. Within three weeks she'd gained back five pounds, the color had returned to her face, and the dark circles under her eyes were fading. For the first time in months she seemed happy.

From this time forward she accepted me not only as her brother, but as "her spiritual brother," because the presence of God had become an absorbing new dimension in her life. We began reading *The Daily Word*, a nondenominational booklet with prayers and quotes from the Scriptures. Lana wouldn't let a day go by without reading its inspirational message. In the weeks and months that followed, whenever I stayed overnight I would awaken to find one of her sweet, loving "good morning" notes placed near my bed where I'd be sure to see it first thing.

One day she surprised me by announcing, "I'm getting ready for my comeback." She did a little dance as she spoke these words, but I sensed a seriousness in her words.

Within days we were busy doing what we always did at the beginning of some new enterprise. This time we were devising a new beauty makeover for Lana's reemergence into the world of the living. Ever so slightly, I changed the color of her famous hair, adding a subtle luminescence to the formula—"Champagne blond" we called it. The color delighted Lana. Her new makeup adjustments were soft and flattering. I moved the rouge slightly lower on her cheeks and began using a new palette of pale, coral shades to give her a healthier, *outdoors* look. Lana bubbled over with plans for her "comeback," an expression she'd never liked in the past but now openly embraced. She was starting life anew.

Now, after years of deliberation and no small amount of procrastination, she decided to finally write her autobiography with the help of a ghostwriter. She also instructed her agents to arrange television guest appearances, as long as they were on "a well-established series" and "starring roles."

In countless interviews to come and an extensive article in *People* magazine, Lana publicly credited me with saving her life. She went so far as to say she thought I had been an instrument of God. Her gratitude for my helping to bring about the miraculous turnaround in her life never wavered. Her loving handwritten notes to me continued throughout the next decade.

Our first steps back into the limelight were tentative. Lana wanted people to know she'd returned from the brink and felt great. She suggested we go out dancing. As a former Fred Astaire/Arthur Murray dance instructor, that suited me.

Acutely aware of the importance of maintaining her newly recovered strength, I insisted that evenings include a healthy meal. Soon we were seen everywhere—at Le Dôme, La Masia, Spago. The Bistro Garden, Jimmy's, and Nicky Blair's. Nicky, who adored Lana, asked her one evening if he could summon a photographer to take her picture. She said yes, and in no time word spread among members of the paparazzi that Lana Turner was back. She even managed to be on time for several important functions, never failing to look her glamorous best.

All in all, we experienced an incredible conclusion to a year that had begun under black clouds of anxiety and fear. Lana, definitely on a roll, enjoyed every minute of it, as did I. Little did either of us know what awaited us just around the corner.

⌁ 11 ⌁

Comeback

1 9 8 1

*C*ontinuing her treatment with Dr. Khalsa, Lana improved rapidly and felt good enough to begin her autobiography. She put any number of potential ghostwriters through the wringer before finding one she could work with—sort of. I'm sure she drove the poor guy up the wall as their sessions together stretched into several months, six to eight hours a day.

Lana improved so much that she accepted an invitation as a guest of honor at the Deauville Film Festival in September 1981. She would join directors Arthur Hiller and Joseph L. Mankiewicz in France to receive this most coveted and prestigious award. She told me it would be the *first* major appearance of her *comeback*. Knowing that I'd never been to France, Lana went out of her way to plan some special things for me. I was floored when she said, "Dear brother, we will leave a few days early. You'll love Paris."

And love it I did! Paris turned out to be everything I'd ever dreamed it to be, and then some.

Lana expressed a desire to keep a low profile until she unveiled "the new me" in Deauville. We stayed in an elegant hotel on the Champs-Elysées. The windows of our suite opened to a breathtaking view of the Arc de Triomphe. We attracted little attention as we strolled the Left Bank along the River Seine.

On one day we visited boutiques on the Rue St. Honoré and in the evening drove to the outskirts of town where we had dinner in a marvelous restaurant. Lana's makeup and evening attire were impeccable. Other diners smiled but did not intrude or cause any fuss. Despite the absence of press, we were treated to a royal repast, compliments of the management.

The following day, rested and relaxed, and both of us dressed to perfection, we entered our limousine for the drive to Deauville. En route, Lana complained that her beautiful "Century City tan" had lost its glow. "It's fading. People will think I've been ill."

"Lana," I assured her, "you look divine."

"Well, I've tried to improve it, but the stuff didn't work."

I gulped. "What *stuff*, Lana?"

"Oh, I put on some *tan enhancer* back at the hotel."

"You did *what?*" I envisioned all my long hours of work on her face disappearing in blisters and burns.

"Don't get so excited. It didn't work. I should have known anything with the name *Indian Earth* wouldn't give me a suntan."

Well, I thought, *if it doesn't work, no harm done.* I later learned that Lana failed to read the instructions, which clearly stated the product would take effect *gradually.*

As we sped along the highway, I spent my time gazing out the window at the beautiful French countryside and didn't pay much attention to Lana. I finally turned to her, intending to call her attention to an old farmhouse up ahead. When I saw her, though, I was speechless. The *Indian Earth* obviously did work, because her face had taken on a deep *bronze* shade.

Startled, she said, "What's wrong? Are you all right, Eric?"

I gulped again. "Lana," I said slowly, "your face looks kind of . . . *dark.*"

"How dark???"

"Well, just dark." I didn't want to say, "You now have a rusty *orange* complexion."

Lana's face shaded over in fear, and her eyes narrowed as she quickly removed a compact from her purse. For a moment she studied her reflection in the mirror and then snapped the compact shut.

"Oh my God, Eric, I can't arrive looking like this." By now her voice was several pitches higher.

To this day I'm grateful she did not panic. Instead, the incident struck her as hysterically funny. We both started to laugh.

"Instead of Lana Turner, I'll be arriving as Pocahontas!" she giggled, vigorously rubbing her cheeks with a tissue. But nothing happened. The weird color resisted removal. If anything, the bronze became bronzier. "Well, I'm not letting anyone see me this way," she declared. The laughter ceased and I could see we might be in for trouble after all.

Luckily, our chauffeur spoke recognizable English and seemed to know what Lana needed. He found a neighborhood gas station in a little town and pulled off the road so the glamorous American cinema star Lana Turner might slip unnoticed into the tiny loo to scrub the *Indian Earth* off her face. I waited, and waited, and waited. Finally, after fifteen minutes, Lana emerged, her face glowing like polished copper. It took all I could do to control my amusement.

Lana was not at all amused. "Eric! I can't get this shit off! What am I going to do?"

She then insisted that I come into the small ladies' room with her and work some kind of magic. She pulled. I resisted. Worried that we would soon draw a crowd, I followed her. The poor chauffeur, waving his hands to a gathering group of villagers, tried to explain our predicament and "strange American customs."

Lana Turner fans suddenly seemed to be coming out of the woodwork. She'd always been popular in France and within a few moments of my being tugged by Lana into the small facility, a good-sized crowd from this very small town had assembled. I peeked out and saw them surrounding the limousine, exclaiming, "Mon Dieu, Lana Turner!"

Inside, we took desperate measures. I think Lana would have taken on steel wool if she thought it might help. Lana never used soap because of its drying qualities, but I insisted we give the soap dispenser, mounted by the sink, a try. Gently, I helped massage the goo into her cheeks, forehead, neck, and chin. Miracle of miracles, her color returned to normal. That done, she began the hourlong process of reapplying her makeup. At my urging, she put on the finishing touches in the limo as we rolled on toward Deauville. Relieved, I leaned back and enjoyed a glass of French champagne. I began to chuckle and within seconds both of us were laughing so hard our sides ached. We'd been through such a ludicrous scene. We arrived in Deauville with Lana's eyes filled with tears of laughter.

"Dammit," she said, dabbing lightly at her eyes with a tissue, "now I'm going to have eye makeup runing down my face!" However, her tissue dabbing forestalled that possible catastrophe.

We arrived at the Hotel Royale on "Lana Turner

time," one hour and a half late. Lana, every inch the movie queen, stepped gracefully from the limousine into a barrage of reporters and flashing cameras. Her radiant face reflected the first of numerous moments of glory she would experience during our stay in Deauville.

Inside the hotel lobby we encountered a second crush of press, French dignitaries and diplomats, fans and celebrities—among them, Leslie Caron and the king of pop art, Andy Warhol. After a proper period of meeting and being met, Lana suggested we go up to our rooms. In the elevator Andy Warhol leaned over and asked Lana if he could do a painting of her. She may have been vaguely aware of his prized "one of a kind" portraits of Elizabeth Taylor, Liza Minnelli, and so many others. She certainly knew of his Campbell's Soup Can artwork, and considered them slightly less than art and outrageously priced. But she pretended to be flattered and gave her approval.

Lana thought of Warhol as a strange and grotesque apparition whose appearance bordered on ghoulish. Several months later he sent her the completed portrait as a gift, an *original* one and only Lana Turner silkscreen on canvas by Warhol. I thought it was outstanding, a unique version of the "later" Lana, done in the master's famed primary colors and out-of-register style. Lana hated it. "It makes me look too severe and hard."

On the evening of the Deauville reception, the

grand ballroom overflowed with lavish floral arrangements and hundreds of dignitaries from the international film community. When Lana made her entrance the paparazzi surrounded us once more. I could see that Lana had begun to tire. She found posing for flash photos exhausting and hard on her eyes. I turned and whispered in her ear, "Give them the Gloria Swanson look from *Sunset Boulevard*."

Lana did a great impression of Swanson from that film. She winked at me, moved back a few steps, straightened herself to her full height of five feet, four inches (plus high heels), and gave them Norma Desmond, stopping just short of comic parody. The crowd went wild and for several more minutes the strobes and flashbulbs popped.

I moved in and surrounded her with a protective hug and steered the two of us toward the dining area. Six burly security guards joined in and protected us all the way to our table.

Leslie Caron, whom Lana had known at MGM, and Yves Montand were seated with us. A charming Montand kissed Lana's hand and complimented her gown. He captivated her immediately. She loved gallantry and manners. I sat to Lana's left and Leslie Caron sat to my left. Sean Connery, on Lana's right, had costarred with her in one of his earliest films, *Another Time, Another Place*. Lana reportedly picked the relatively unknown Connery to be her leading man over nine more qualified contenders.

In her book, *Detour*, Cheryl, Lana's daughter, suggested that the crew working on the film with Lana and Sean were pretty sure the two were having an affair until Johnny Stompanato arrived in England to break it up. When Stompanato confronted Connery on the set and threatened him, Sean promptly decked Lana's gigolo.

Less than a year later Sean Connery attended the Academy Awards in Hollywood and sat at Lana's table the night she lost the Best Actress award nomination for *Peyton Place* to Joanne Woodward, who won for *The Three Faces of Eve*. Stompanato threw a fit because Lana had refused his services as an escort to the awards ceremony. She never appeared at another public event with him and a few days later, on Good Friday, Johnny's blood-splattered body was found decorating Lana's bedroom, thus launching one of the greatest scandals in show business history.

So, twenty-three years later, Lana and Sean were once again sharing the same table at an awards ceremony. This time a decidedly chilly air crossed between the two. Cold cordiality was the best the Englishman offered the legendary movie queen. Lana gave back what she got.

Placing a napkin over her mouth, Lana whispered to me, "Who put a bug up his ass?"

I shrugged. Personally I thought the actor could have shown some respect to the woman who had given him a career boost back in 1957. I later found myself in the men's room, two urinals away from Connery. I introduced myself. "How do you do, Mr. Connery. I'm with—"

"Call me Sean," he interrupted. "Yes, I know. You're here with Lana Turner."

"I understand, Mr. Connery . . . Sean . . . your first big break came in Lana's picture, *Another Time, Another Place.*"

"Wrong!" he declared, showing some irritation. "It was my first part in an *American* film. I'd worked in many English pictures."

"But I understand," I continued, "that Lana chose you over better known American actors who were up for the part."

"So?" he replied, indignant. I knew there was nothing else to say.

A few minutes later, back at our table, Connery's expression resembled that of a baby's rash. I related my earlier conversation with him to Lana. Anger clouded her face. "I don't know what his problem is other than the fact he's such an asshole," she said softly, disguising her anger by feigning a smile. "He's another one with an enormous ego and a rotten temper"—I immediately thought of her experience with Richard Burton—"but we're going to have a fabulous evening, aren't we? And forget Mr. Connery."

She meant it, and we did. To the delight of the Fourth Estate, we stepped out onto the floor and danced the night away.

Two evenings later the festival honored Lana with a screening of *The Postman Always Rings Twice*, considered by many critics to be Lana's most remembered performance. Following the movie, Lana, dressed in a red silk pantsuit with plunging neckline, delighted the assemblage of her peers (and critics) with a wonderfully down-to-earth speech. No one would ever upstage Lana when she felt up to it—and she felt up to it that night.

We stayed on for a couple more days so Lana could rest up and then flew back to Los Angeles, where she would soon be making a guest appearance in an episode of "Falcon Crest," one of the most popular prime-time soaps.

Lana wanted to work. It didn't matter to her that she would be acting for the small screen. The important thing was being before the *camera*. A big television fan, and familiar with the new trend in prime-time soaps, she saw nothing wrong with television provided, of course, that she receive the respect and treatment deserving a star of her magnitude, and she approached the series with cautious optimism.

Jane Wyman, the series' star, had a lot of sway, but the producers had already indicated that if Lana's appearance came off well, she would be invited back on a semiregular basis.

The perks were impressive, considering the fast-paced world of television. Lana received prominent guest-star billing, a chauffeur-driven limousine to take her to and from the studio, and a special dressing room trailer of her own. Unlike her previous two films shot mostly on location, she would again be working before the cameras inside a major studio with state-of-the-art lighting and cinematography.

Lana's vanity nearly caused a tragedy. She'd decided to have some cosmetic surgery done on her face. That frightened me, and I warned her to be careful.

"All I want done, darling, is a little tuck around the eyes," she explained, referring to her upper lids and the bags under her eyes. "It's no big deal."

"Then do me a favor. Don't just run your fingers through the Yellow Pages looking for a surgeon."

"Oh no, darling. Don't worry about that. I've already chosen someone. He's been recommended by a friend."

When I learned the doctor's name, I knew I'd heard it before and his reputation hadn't been presented as sterling. "Lana, get at least three consultations before you have this work done. Remember, dear, this is your face we're talking about."

She ignored my advice. "Eric, you worry too much. Why should I have to see three doctors when one is all it takes?" Lana always preferred someone recommended from "the inside." She abhorred any scrutiny by "total strangers."

On the appointed day for the operation I picked her up at her condo, delivered her to the doctor's office on Sunset Boulevard, and came back afterward to drive her home. Within a few weeks Lana's eye job looked to me like a disaster in the making. Even she had to see the unsatisfactory results.

In removing the lower bags, the doctor had created a severe downward crease just below the inner corner of her right eye. It was painfully noticeable, and it would remain so. Many frustrating hours in the makeup chair would be required later to properly camouflage the highly visible flaw.

Furious over what she considered serious damage to her famous face, Lana called the doctor a *butcher* and threatened a lawsuit. She later decided not to pursue the matter because of possible public embarrassment.

Despite her cosmetic problems, work on "Falcon Crest" progressed rapidly. She professed liking the speed of television, as she could no longer physically deal with the long and demanding hours on the set.

Lana became a night owl, often watching television until four in the morning. In order to make it to the set for her six o'clock call, she had to stay up all night and would arrive exhausted from lack of sleep, then have to wait around for hours in her dressing room, fully made up, until needed. Her close-ups were often not filmed until after nine in the evening. After waiting ten to twelve hours, she knew she wouldn't look her best and it outraged her that the production company gave so little consideration to her needs. When she was finally called to the set, she deliberately kept everyone waiting by insisting on redoing her makeup one final time. I could do nothing to smooth over the situation.

All was forgiven when Lana's first appearance on "Falcon Crest" turned out to be a major success, with ratings for her episode among the highest the show had ever received. Soon the producers were calling and asking her to return as Jacqueline Perrault, her character, for six more episodes next season.

Lana was thrilled. Her successful guest appearance boosted her confidence, and she felt she had accomplished another step in her "comeback."

Lana's reemergence into the limelight was not without its comical moments, however. I remember one particular evening when we were on our way to one of Debbie Reynolds's star-studded charity events at Pips, a popular private club in Beverly Hills. I was driving Lana in my sparkling new apricot-colored Bricklin, which had doors that lifted straight up like a De Lorean.

Impeccably dressed and late as usual, we pulled into the driveway just as a pack of photographers surged toward us to get a closer look at the occupants of this jazzy vehicle. Even though Lana always preferred me to get her door, a valet was already approaching her side of the car. I pushed the button to release the doors. Nothing happened. I tried again. Still nothing.

The serenely poised look on Lana's face melted as

she shot me a look of irritation. "What's the matter? Open the door."

"I can't. The button isn't working," I responded meekly.

"What? Eric, do something!" She was starting to panic.

"I'm trying."

"Well, try harder. We can't just sit here!"

There was a conspicuous buzz from the gathering crowd of fans, newsmen, and photographers surrounding the car, wondering why glamorous Lana Turner and her stalwart companion were not getting out.

"Shit! I'm getting claustrophobia!" Lana hissed through clenched teeth as the photographers pressed against the glass, catching her stricken expression from angles that could only be unflattering fodder for the tabloids.

I kept pushing buttons and, while I was having no luck with the doors, the windows finally went down. At least we were making progress. I looked at Lana and smiled.

"The windows may be down, but that doesn't get me out of here," she said. "Dammit, Eric, look at the paparazzi gawking at me!"

"They're not gawking at you, they're gawking at my car!" I shot back.

"Bullshit! They're trying to catch me in an awkward situation."

As people peered through her window, Lana's

eyes grew larger. She began to twist and squirm in her seat.

"What are you doing?" I asked.

"I'm going to crawl out!" She somehow managed to turn herself around with her knees in the seat and stick her rear end out the open window. The valets tactfully grabbed her around the waist and gently pulled her out of the car. Through this entire operation her heavily sprayed hair never moved.

Since my six-foot, four-inch frame made a similar exit impossible, she left me sitting in the car and allowed herself to be escorted inside without me. I remained in the Bricklin for several minutes, continuing to push buttons and fiddle with anything else that might work. Suddenly, the doors popped open and I was free!

When I entered the club I saw Lana mingling with a group that included Debbie Reynolds, Rita Hayworth, and Mac Krim. Instead of joining her, I headed straight for the bar and ordered a triple vodka. A short time later I glanced over at Lana. She was looking at me and gesturing with her little finger, motioning me to come to her. The expression on her face said, "I'm sorry." I gave her a smile and started toward her. All was forgiven.

Shooting was about to start up again for the new season of "Falcon Crest." From the day Lana signed to do the series, rumors of a feud between Lana and Jane Wyman began to circulate. They were not entirely unfounded. Wyman, an Academy

Award-winning actress from the old school, had a reputation for professionalism, for being on time, for never holding up production. She also enjoyed being the highest salaried woman on television. Never considered a "glamour girl," she found it difficult to put up with the pampered treatment Lana expected.

One day between setups I left Lana, who was fussing with her makeup, and wandered over to Jane Wyman's trailer. We chatted for a few minutes and I soon found myself styling and combing one of her wigs. "Nobody can do this wig like you," she said.

"Thank you." I drank in the compliment. "But Jane, these bangs make you look like Mamie Eisenhower." We both started to laugh.

"Then do something about it," she replied.

I knew I had to be careful because hairdressers on the show were part of a very strong union and didn't cotton much to outsiders. Lana had to obtain special permission to have me on the set as her personal stylist; still, a union hairdresser got screen credit. Lana could easily have gotten me into the union but chose not to. I don't think she wanted me to achieve that kind of recognition within the industry. It might take me away from her.

I stopped fiddling with Jane's wig and told her I would have to return to Lana because she might need me at any moment.

"So what?" she said.

"Jane, she's been my friend for many years."

On my return to Lana's dressing room I made the mistake of mentioning Jane Wyman's interest in having me do her wigs. She blew sky-high.

"That bitch! How dare she try to use you? She has her own hairdresser to fluff those damned wigs! You are *my* hairdresser, exclusively," she ranted, pointing her finger directly in my face, "and don't you ever forget it!"

Because of her tardiness and temperamental demands, Lana did not endear herself to the "Falcon Crest" crew. Her six guest appearances scheduled for the following season were reduced to four. During the season finale, a major character on the show went berserk and started shooting a pistol in all directions. Lana and most of the series' regulars were in the line of fire. After this shocking "cliff-hanger" the public would have to wait until the next season to find out who lived or died. Even the writers were unsure at this point.

Jane Wyman had the last word. In a meeting with the Lorimar brass, she had input in discussions about the story line for the upcoming season. When it came time to discuss whether Lana's character should return, the question became Jane's to answer. Without anger or lengthy explanations, she reportedly had only one word to say: *no.* So, Lana "died!"

Although the "Falcon Crest" experience may have taken its toll on all concerned, it paled in comparison to the challenge she and I were about to face.

Between Lana's two seasons on the series, her tell-all autobiography had finally hit the bookstores. Of course, a high-profile celebrity book doesn't just sell itself. The celebrity does. Lana would be the centerpiece of a mammoth promotional campaign arranged by her publishers.

We were about to hit the road again.

⚝ 12 ⚝

The Legend, the Lady, the Book Tour

1982

E. P. Dutton and Company published *Lana: The Legend, the Lady, the Truth*, Lana's eagerly awaited autobiography, in 1982. Such a celebrity event required Lana endure an extensive, arduous book tour of major markets from New York to Los Angeles. Lana's new status as a television star on one of the hottest prime-time series could only enhance book sales in cities where she appeared.

Anyone who has never done a book tour is in for a shock. Even movie stars with junkets to accompany the opening of their latest films cannot be prepared for the manner in which they will be received on tour, or the heavy schedule of book signings, interviews, radio and television shows, and anything else the publisher can throw in to hype the book.

In her best businesswoman mode, Lana orchestrated every detail and dictated where she would or would not go and what she would or would not do.

Only a legend could get away with making such restrictions on her publisher. In great form, her health still improving, she looked wonderful and had not gone back to her vodka.

I would accompany her, so I shuffled my appointments and blocked myself "out" of my salon for three weeks. Lana busied herself with having an entirely new wardrobe created for the occasion, composed principally of smart, sharply tailored suits. Several evening gowns and cocktail dresses were added for good measure. Her accessories would be augmented with several important pieces of jewelry from her priceless collection.

Our stops would include scheduled book signings, local radio and television interviews and a great deal of national TV coverage once we arrived in New York.

Instructions for our public appearances had been drilled into me long before the tour began. Lana handled that chore herself with loving patience, but her rules were written in blood. For instance, Lana would never under any circumstances allow a security man or chauffeur to open her limousine door. "You get out and open it for me, darling."

Since I always sat to her left, on the traffic side, that meant I would open my door into the street. Lana would quickly add, "And don't forget to look both ways when you get out."

I never quite ascertained whether her warning emanated from concern for my safety or as insurance to avoid embarrassment and inconvenience to Lana should I suddenly be struck by a car and fail to open her door, or a combination of both. Either way, it's always nice to believe you're indispensable.

"Walk *calmly* around the rear of the limo," she cautioned, "reach *calmly* for my door and open it. *Calmly.*"

"Yes, Lana, I think I've got it. *Calmly.*"

"Remember, dear, my right leg comes out first. Make absolutely sure my right leg comes out and I extend my right hand before you reach down to assist me. Wait until I put my hand in yours, then gently pull me up toward you. But don't pull too fast or use too much strength. *Gently.*"

Rehearsals for these events always made me nervous. Lana insisted she be presented properly, that she exit her limousine like visiting royalty. There could be *no* mistakes.

Once while I was escorting her to a particular book signing several security men suddenly flanked us as we entered a department store. One of them, in an effort to get closer to Lana, kept bumping me and almost knocked me into her.

Lana's swift response: "If that fuckhead bumps you again, just turn to the asshole and say, 'Excuse me, but I am escorting Miss Turner, not you!' "

I relayed her words verbatim to the rude officer. "But," he objected, "security is essential." That's when Lana interceded.

"Excuse me," she said in a voice of velvet and ice,

"you are strictly a *hired* security guard. This tall, blond gentleman is my very close *personal* friend. *He* is escorting me, and don't you forget it."

The guard immediately fell back to a respectable distance. Later, when we were alone, Lana went off on a tirade about untrained security and inefficient department store personnel. "They all want to get close, to touch me, to take hold of my hand, to stare at me. They try to get too familiar, and I *can't* stand it. If anyone ever tries to bump you out of the way again, you tell them to go to hell!"

I knew the *real* reasons Lana disliked anyone coming too close. Coiffed and made up flawlessly, she didn't want to be mussed or disheveled, and loathed people who stared into her face. She also had an obsessive fear of catching germs from strangers. But, most importantly, she lived in daily fear that one of Stompanato's mobster pals would slide up next to her and shove a knife between her ribs.

For public book signings, Lana always insisted on sitting behind a large desk on a raised platform, so she could keep an eye on everyone and everything. Such a setting prevented the public from getting too close.

To avoid the possibility of bomb threats or other problems, strict security procedures had to be letter perfect and followed without deviation. Customers who purchased her book found themselves waiting in long lines to obtain her autograph. They approached the dais and their books were given first to a security guard, who flipped the pages and assured himself there were no dangers hidden between the pages. The guard then passed the book to me, and I passed it on to Lana. She signed each book, "Sincerely, Lana Turner." The message never wavered. Personal inscriptions or messages of any kind were omitted. Then she would look up, smile or offer a polite "thank you," and hand the book across the table to the customer.

I remember one incident in New York City. We were en route to Macy's. Lana had spent part of the day doing radio and television interviews. On each show she plugged her book autographing schedule. She still wore her TV makeup and one of her trademark suits.

Two blocks away from Macy's I noticed a great mass of people swarming over the street, in effect, blocking our way. "Lana, something's wrong. Maybe there's a fire or some kind of emergency," I said, worried that Lana would be blamed if we arrived late.

"Fire?" she exclaimed, looking up from her compact with a start. Then a sly, knowing smile spread across her face. "That's not a fire, my darling brother. They're waiting for *me*." And so they were.

Once inside, the signing went smoothly. Hundreds, perhaps thousands, were lined up throughout the store, down the block, and around the block. I thought to myself, *New York loves Lana*.

Suddenly, a piercing male voice rang out above

the noisy crowd. "You *murderer!*" I caught a brief glimpse of the long-haired man who had shouted the accusation as three policemen tackled the fellow to the ground and took him away.

Lana's panic-stricken expression is frozen forever in my memory. She slowly put down her pen, turned toward me and the store detectives behind her, and said, "That's it. We're outta here!"

I felt sorry for all those fans waiting for Lana to sign their books, but my fear of someone killing Lana took precedence over all else.

The now welcome security staff formed a tight circle around us to lead us to a private office. Instead, Lana directed them outside, where our limousine awaited our departure. We were swiftly swooped out of the store and into the limousine, and the driver was instructed to return us to our hotel immediately.

The incident so disarmed Lana that she canceled most of the remaining dates of the tour and made preparations to come home to California.

"I tell you, Eric, they're going to get me one of these days. I know it!" she said firmly.

The hundreds of people waiting in line at Macy's with their newly purchased books had no idea what happened, or that Lana had left the building and would not be returning.

⊰ 13 ⊱

Lana and Cheryl: Imitation of Life

1982

> How about a mother's love? By telephone, by postcard, by magazine interview— you've given me everything *but yourself*!
> —Sandra Dee to Lana
> Turner in *Imitation of Life*

"She's a selfish bitch!" Lana said, slamming down a stack of papers and rising from her desk.

"Who?" I asked, setting down my bags. It was a warm afternoon in 1982. I'd just arrived, so she caught me completely off guard—no greeting, no pleasantries, just red-in-the-face fury.

"Cheryl!" she shouted. "She's done it again!"

Oh, I thought. *Nothing new.* These two were always at it about something. "What's the problem now?" I removed my jacket and tossed it over the back of a chair.

"She refused to sign the damned release!"

Ah, the release. Here we go again. Warner Bros. had just optioned Lana's autobiography for a television Movie of the Week. I'd attended numerous meetings with Lana and Warner Bros. executives who were trying to find a screenwriter acceptable to Lana for the project. Without Cheryl's permission to use her name in the film, there was little chance that the proposed picture would ever be made, and Cheryl refused to grant it.

"Unbelievable," Lana said. She lit a cigarette, sat on the edge of a chair, inhaled deeply, and then dramatically tossed her head back and belched the smoke upward. Bette Davis could not have done it better.

I'd grown to know Cheryl somewhat and, despite Lana's bitterness and present anger, I thought I understood Cheryl's reluctance to accommodate her mother. She probably didn't feel like having the Johnny Stompanato murder and her role in it dredged up for a vehicle that could only glorify her famous mother.

I also knew Lana. Any movie based on her own book would paint her as the caring mother who stood by her guilty daughter during a time of crisis. Lana would make sure of that. I believed Cheryl saw through all of the hype and simply didn't want any part of it.

"She's an ungrateful bitch!" Lana continued, exhaling another billow of smoke. I expected a long tongue of fire to follow. I couldn't recall ever seeing her so angry.

"Lana," I said, attempting to soothe her feelings, "how can you say that? She's your own flesh and blood."

"Bullshit! That's not my blood. My blood is warm. She's a cold-blooded bitch!" I could see an ugly scene in the offing.

"What do you mean, not your blood?" I asked. It had never occurred to me that Cheryl might be adopted. Had she been?

Lana surely saw the confusion in my face. "I mean," she said, "it's not *my* blood. Therefore she is not my daughter."

"I don't follow."

"They removed all of *my* blood from her at the hospital," she explained, referring to her difficulties giving birth to Cheryl, who entered the world with the dread Rh factor, requiring numerous blood transfusions. "My blood," Lana continued, "had to be all drained out of her and replaced with someone else's—totally." She reached for her glass of vodka and cranberry juice, sipped and paused as if probing for a reason to justify her declaration. "God only knows *whose* blood is in her veins, but it sure as hell isn't mine!"

I listened, stunned into silence, scarcely believing her words, wondering how a mother could say such things about her own flesh and blood. Lana seemed poised at the threshold of some personal hell, battling unknown demons.

Finally I found my voice. "But Lana," I argued, "you carried her inside *your* body. She's part of you. She'll always be a part of you."

Lana made a sort of "hmmph" sound as if to dismiss a technicality. I sensed her rage subsiding.

"Maybe she'll change her mind," I said calmly, hoping to diffuse her anger.

Her half-closed eyelids told me the discussion had ended. She would repeat the tirade about "the blood" many times during our years together, especially whenever Cheryl annoyed or openly defied her.

Hours later, after she calmed down, she broached the subject in a more sane and rational tone of voice. "I've thought about what you said. Of course she's my daughter by birth. Maybe you're right. Maybe she will change her mind. We'll have to wait and see, won't we?"

The storm had passed—for the moment. Cheryl, indeed her mother's daughter, with Lana's iron will, never did sign that release. The issue would remain a bone of contention throughout the rest of Lana's life.

$\mathcal{A}$bout ten years before I met Lana, I'd seen three of her most successful pictures: *Peyton Place*, *Imitation of Life*, and *Portrait in Black*. In these films she played mothers with troubled teenage daughters. These pictures opened the door to a new phase of her career, attracting a second generation audience. The baby-boomer parents related to Lana's sudsy melodramas in which most problems were resolved with the hope of a rosy future by the final credits. Not a true picture of the real world, of course.

The films Lana made during this resurgence of her career became modern-day escapism for moviegoers, a return to the uplifting pictures of the depressed 1930s.

Peyton Place, the biggest grossing film of 1957, earned Lana that Best Actress Oscar nomination. Although the picture had been completed months before the Stompanato murder, it paralleled many of the difficulties Lana was currently experiencing with teenage Cheryl.

In her autobiography, *Detour*, Cheryl described how stunned she'd been when she saw *Peyton Place*. Watching her mother's cold, calculated manner in dealing with her screen daughter, she quickly grasped the all-too-familiar scenario. The scenes reflected exactly the way Lana *acted* during their private confrontations. On-screen or off, just another magnificent performance from a brilliant actress.

Imitation of Life, in which a mother and daughter are in love with the same man, and *Portrait in Black*, in which Lana played a murderess, were lavish Ross Hunter productions drenched in glamour and sophistication, designer gowns and expensive jewels.

Sandra Dee, a former child model, who was enjoying great popularity at the time (and who would later marry singer Bobby Darin), played Lana's daughter in the former film and her stepdaughter in the latter. Ironically, she and Cheryl were the same age.

$\mathscr{P}$rior to my 1972 arrival in California and being seduced into the private world of Lana Turner, I'd read numerous magazine articles extolling the wonderful and harmonious relationship between Lana and Cheryl following their involvement in "Hollywood's Greatest Scandal." Lana had only recently been quoted as saying, "All is warm and wonderful between my daughter and myself."

Whenever I find myself wondering how the public can be so gullible about real life compared to the "reel" world of motion pictures, I expect to find Lana and Cheryl embroiled in nothing more than normal mother-and-daughter differences, enjoying a world of perfection that only money could afford. I often recall my own naiveté in coming to Hollywood.

Lana's Pacific Palisades penthouse, overlooking the beach in Santa Monica, created the perfect setting for rich, luxurious, carefree living. God knows Lana had the wardrobe and jewelry. The missing element? No Sandra Dee. The empty chair at the table belonged to an absent Cheryl. Mother and daughter were not enjoying an idyllic relationship. They rarely spoke.

I've come to believe, as many of Lana's friends and business associates so often suggested, that Lana never should have become a mother. She had no time for the true meaning of "home life," always too preoccupied with the larger-than-life image of her screen persona, created by the legendary Louis B. Mayer.

I can't say she didn't love Cheryl. She did, as much as Lana could love anyone beyond herself. I think she carried on a love/hate relationship with her own ego because of her inability to exhibit emotional love—except on the screen. Lana didn't know how to handle a nurturing, compassionate relationship with her daughter, nor did she with any of her husbands. There always existed some underlying tension, some sense of competing with those who came too close to the frightened child behind the glitz and glamour of "celebrity."

Cheryl wanted more from her mother than Lana was capable of giving. Lana could not give up being the "Love Goddess" to the world in order to be a loving wife and mother. She'd been programmed otherwise by the moguls of money-making.

Cheryl had not been a deprived child, however. She'd never lacked for comfort or luxury (or surrogate mothers and a catalog of "father" figures). As Lana saw it, she'd taken much "valuable time" away from her demanding career (and social life) to be with "my little girl." She had that in common with Joan Crawford, whose daughter, Christina, like

Cheryl, would write books to show her "ingratitude." The valuable time Lana bemoaned usually benefited her more than Cheryl. It often involved taking Cheryl on visits and afternoon adventures that were nothing more than photo sessions for fan magazines to build Lana's image as a "good mother."

By the mid-1970s that superficial closeness between mother and daughter ceased to exist. There were no more photo sessions, no more loving quotes. Their relationship had, in fact, deteriorated into an occasional, carefully worded press release.

I can't recall Cheryl ever being present during the dozens of trips I made to Lana's Pacific Palisades apartment, nor did I ever see her at Lana's Ivory Tower in Century City. She became conspicuous, to me, by her absence.

One afternoon Cheryl phoned her mother while we were watching some inane soap opera. Their conversation was brief and ended with, "I'm having my hair done. I don't have time to talk."

I asked Lana why Cheryl never came around and she said, "We talk on the phone."

"Don't you see each other?"

She looked up into the mirror at my reflection. "Infrequently," she said, closing the subject.

There'd been a chasm between them for a long time. I didn't know if the Stompanato matter had anything to do with it, but I did know that Lana had some problems with Cheryl's lifestyle. Before I heard it from anyone else, Lana sat me down one day and candidly told me about Cheryl's lesbian relationship with Joyce "Josh" LeRoy.

The irritation in her voice let me know she disapproved of Cheryl's lifestyle. Only later did I come to realize that Lana's distaste had nothing to do with Cheryl's lesbianism. Her main concern, I learned, had to do with adverse publicity, both for Cheryl and for herself. After a career filled with tawdry headlines, I believe she feared her daughter's alternative lifestyle would again show Lana up to the world as a bad mother.

I did see Cheryl at Lana's apartment once—or rather, I *almost* saw her. It happened on Mother's Day, and for the life of me I can't recall the year. My sister, Harriet, and I were in the kitchen stuffing cabbage when the doorbell rang.

We could hear Lana and someone having a conversation that soon escalated into a screaming match between Lana and another female voice. "Get the hell out and don't come back—ever!" Lana's voice screeched, and then I heard the loud slamming of her door.

I left the kitchen to see if Lana needed anything. She was standing in the living room, looking out through her picture window toward the ocean.

"Are you all right?" I asked.

"Damn her!" she said.

I waited.

"The only time she comes around is when she wants something."

"Who, Lana?" I asked.

"Who else? My ingrate daughter. It's Mother's Day. Did she bring a gift or flowers, or a card? She wanted *me* to give *her* something. Can you believe it? On Mother's Day she asks *me* for money."

Shrugging, I uttered something like, "Kids . . ."

"Well," she bit down on her words, "she'll not get a penny from me. Not one red cent!"

I believe I first met Cheryl when she and Josh had a place in Calabasas, on the western end of the San Fernando Valley. A friend and I drove out to see them once without Lana. We seemed to hit it off. I found both women to be bright, attractive, and sophisticated. I liked them. I believe Lana's mother, Mildred, Cheryl's beloved "Gran," lived with them at the time.

No matter what my first impressions were, I can now see that Cheryl and I had no chance of becoming close friends. Lana wouldn't have tolerated it. I *belonged* to Lana and she didn't share her "belongings." Not even with her daughter. I would belong to Lana first, last, and always. Lana preferred that Cheryl and I not be friends.

However, in fairness to Lana, she did make an effort to establish some kind of relationship with Cheryl during this particular phase of her life. Lana would drive out to Calabasas to visit her mother with hopes of seeing Cheryl as well, only to return home disappointed. "She knew I was coming and she purposely left before I arrived. Why does she hurt me this way?" Lana would say.

On other visits to her mother, Lana would return home and I could see that look of hurt and disappointment and the tears trickling down her face.

"Eric," she'd say, "I know Cheryl was there. I could hear noises in the back of the house. She avoids me." Her mood following such visits would be mercurial, ranging from tears to anger to self-pity. I felt so sorry for her, but theirs was a relationship cemented in past events. It would never change.

What really hurt Lana the most, I believe, is that all of those bad feelings came during a period in her life when she actually had time to make an effort to be a mother. Her movie career had become practically nonexistent, along with her fabled love life. With few outside distractions, she developed an inclination to get to know her daughter. She meant well. I knew that, because I knew Lana Turner. The problem? In attempting to make up for lost time, to be a real mother, she became overly demanding and controlling. She tried to take Cheryl back to her teen years when a mother should have been there to guide and counsel her. Lana's efforts came too late. Cheryl, now a grown woman, did not need Lana's advice. She'd already learned what she needed to know the hard way.

During Lana's waning years there were more hostilities and, yes, moments of truce and periods of reconciliation between Lana and Cheryl. But the die had been cast; the volatile chemistry between the two women did not allow room for friendship. The roots of their love/hate relationship ran deep. It couldn't have been merely Cheryl's lesbianism. Lana numbered thousands of gays among her fans, and had numerous gay friends.

Could it be, as so many suspected, the specter of Johnny Stompanato?

⊰ 14 ⊱

Boss Lady

*W*ith most sincere thanks to Lana Turner, I am still introduced as the "stylist to the stars." I'm certainly not the first, nor will I be the last, hairdresser to be stuck with that innocuous title. I consider myself neither starstruck nor a "fanatic." I'm in the business of making people look their very best at all times and I've yet to meet a celebrity who isn't drawn to that prospect. The fact that I have so many gorgeous people with whom to work is a personal, not a business, plus.

In addition to my society friends in Chicago, New York, and Palm Beach, my clientele has included both famous women *and famous men*: Mae West, Bette Davis, Rhonda Fleming, Patricia Neal, Cary Grant, Morgana King, Johnny Ray, Richard Burton, Rutger Hauer, Beverly Sassoon, and Marilu Henner. But *Lana* always came first.

Years after Lana's romance with Tyrone Power,

and long after his death, actress Linda Christian briefly became a client of mine. I honestly didn't know she had *stolen* Ty from Lana and then married him. When I casually mentioned to Lana that I was on my way to do Linda's hair, she went ballistic.

"If you do that bitch's hair, you're out of my life for good!" Her voice dripped with icy, chilling finality.

"Come on, Lana. Calm down. If you don't want me to do it—I won't."

I regrettably had to call Linda and excuse myself from doing her hair in the future. We still see each other socially. Linda never took it personally. She's an actress. She understood.

It was 1982, and Lana's rejuvenated popularity was soaring as a result of her book and television appearances. So was her ego. But not her generosity. I'd heard stories of her several husbands and numerous lovers who had taken her to the financial cleaners but, considering her lavish lifestyle and lucrative income during my time with her, I saw no excuse for her penny-pinching.

In a word, Lana Turner was *cheap*! In no way, however, did that diminish my love and affection for her. I offer this as a realistic observation. Numerous are the people who would readily agree. During our many years together she never once offered me a raise or even a tip. While my salon prices increased constantly with the cost of living, Lana expected me to charge her the same amount as I had the first time I ever did her hair.

In her lofty world of self-importance, she believed the "perks" from my taking her out in public—limousine service, lavish parties, media attention, and hobnobbing with superstars—more than made up for her reluctance to open up her checkbook. Friendship and her checkbook had nothing in common. Only in love and marriage did she close her eyes to money matters.

After we'd been together for eight or nine years, I had my business manager notify her of an increase in my fees. When I arrived at her condo later that week to give her a perm, you could slice the atmosphere with a bread knife. She was seething. At the end of our conversationless session she handed me a check for my services, looked me coolly in the eye, and said, "Here. Business is business and friendship is friendship."

I glanced somewhat nervously at the amount of the check and was relieved to see she had included the increase. She barely spoke to me for the next several weeks except on matters of business.

Lana may have disliked paying me from her own funds, but she had no problem with her generosity when it came to doing so with other people's money. If she could get me on the payroll of one of her projects, so much the better.

During the 1970s, when Lana went on tour with *The Pleasure of His Company* and *Bell, Book and*

Candle, I didn't go along. I couldn't accompany her on long tours and take care of my Beverly Hills salon at the same time. Compromises had to be made by Lana as well as myself. She insisted, nonetheless, that I fly out every two weeks to cut, trim, and color her hair and groom the many Eva Gabor wigs she wore onstage. I told her I couldn't do that unless I received first-class airfare and hotel accommodations, plus a ''hefty'' fee for each of these ''fly-ins.'' To accept the usual fee would have cost me business from other clients, and I couldn't afford to bankrupt myself, even for Lana.

She worried that she wouldn't be able to get the backers of her show to agree to such extravagance. In that case, I told her, she'd have to get another hairdresser.

''Business, Lana,'' I said, parroting her previous declaration to me, ''is business.''

Within a few days she phoned me to say, ''I have good news for you!''

In an effort to keep their star happy, the producers agreed to pay all my expenses. Soon I settled into a comfortable, jet-set kind of existence. I would fly into the city where Lana happened to be appearing, see the play, and attend a party or have an after-theater supper with her. On Monday, when the theater was dark, we'd sleep in late, I'd do her hair, and we'd spend the rest of the day catching up with each other's lives. I'd book the red eye that night and be back in my salon early Tuesday morning.

Lana's tight pursestrings notwithstanding, she did give me some lovely gifts over the years, usually at Christmas or on my birthday. One of my favorite gifts was the crystal chandelier she selected for my new home.

*L*ana had managed shrewd profit participations on several films she did for producer Ross Hunter and Universal Pictures, particularly *Imitation of Life*. On two occasions I personally saw her receive checks for the film's domestic video and foreign theatrical grosses in the amounts of $25,000 and $100,000, respectively. She received royalty payments for the rest of her life.

An astute businesswoman when it came to negotiating her contracts, Lana could be extremely short-sighted with financial opportunities right under her nose. Her Century City apartment, for example. When the owners of the building announced in 1974 that they were converting to condominiums, Lana bought her beloved Ivory Tower for $73,500. She had one complaint: With only two bedrooms, she would have preferred more space for her furnishings and extensive wardrobe. She could have, and *should* have, bought several other units in the building, including one across the hall from hers, which would have allowed for expansion. Several people urged her to do so, but she didn't listen. Since her death I've been told that her condo is now worth close to a half million dollars.

You'll recall that Lana *hated* the Andy Warhol painting of her. For several years she relegated it to an unimportant spot in her cluttered office, always planning to get rid of it. I knew an art dealer in New York and told Lana I'd have her make some discreet inquiries as to its value. The dealer quickly responded with an offer of $25,000.

I cautioned Lana. ''If they're that anxious, I think you can get a lot more for it. Why don't you wait a while?''

Lana thought that to be a lot of money for such a white elephant and instructed me to accept the deal immediately. Today, with Lana and Andy Warhol both deceased, you can imagine the value of such a painting. The last known asking price was in the vicinity of $350,000.

For some time Lana left her financial matters totally in the hands of a business manager whom she eventually grew to distrust. She ignored friends who urged her to fire him. Lana, a business conservative, often stayed too long with old business associates simply to avoid having to look for someone new. When she finally parted company with the manager, she discovered he'd sold all her shares in Taco Bell without her knowledge or approval, just before the company's merger with PepsiCo. The stock went up considerably in value.

When it came to negotiating a deal for a property in which she took personal interest, like the film rights to her autobiography, Lana could be tough-as-nails and unflinching in her demands—sometimes to her detriment.

One day I rearranged a particularly hectic afternoon so I could drive her out to Warner Bros. The studio had optioned her book for a television movie and meetings had been scheduled to find a suitable screenwriter for the project. She pointedly arrived *on time* for these appointments. Perfectly made up and smartly dressed, she turned heads as we walked into the executive suite. She was selling *Lana Turner*, and she must rule over these proceedings with authority.

Her demands were tough and unrelenting. "Falcon Crest" and the book tour had given her a boost, and she intended to take full advantage of her new financial prestige. She knew that in Hollywood money and position are what it's all about. She had both and wanted more.

"I'm selling you my story with the understanding that I have complete artistic control—screenplay, casting approval, the works," she told them.

They listened.

She didn't like any of the writers the studio offered. Lana interviewed various candidates from around the country and finally asked the head of the story department to find someone from Los Angeles with whom she could work on a regular basis.

The executives were uncomfortable with the prospect of Lana's "participation." They saw it more as her constant interference with the process. Lana wouldn't budge. End of discussion. They scheduled two more meetings. The first was as fruitless as the previous one. On the day of the second meeting Lana phoned me.

Fully aware that she was taking advantage of my time and transportation, she attempted to placate me. "Honey," she said, "I know it's your full day at the salon, but you know how important this is. I do need you to be with me."

She used all her persuasive charm and sincerity to seduce me—successfully, of course. She needed me, but apparently not enough to compensate me for my time or gasoline. Once again my clients, including a large wedding party, were shuffled around so I could take Lana to this final meeting at the studio where her career had begun, and been first rejected, forty-five years ago by Jack Warner.

Inside the same Warner Bros. executive offices, Lana read a few treatments and portions of a completed script for *The Legend, the Lady, the Truth*. She rattled off a long list of criticisms. "The Stompanato incident should be *much* more dramatic, and make the scenes between me and Lex Barker really hot and sexy. He was *Tarzan*, for God's sake, and a tiger! As for the producers, you can make them as evil as possible. The same for some of my costars."

She read more of the material, listened to one writer trying to explain his slant on her story, and suddenly, without warning, jumped up and said, "Eric, let's go!"

"But we're not through yet," said the shaken writer.

"Oh yes, we are," she snapped. "I've heard *enough*. You're not going to trash my story."

I thought that was an odd remark since she had suggested making it more sensational in many places. The writer certainly must have pushed a sensitive button. Again, I wondered: Did it have to do with Johnny Stompanato?

"That's it," she said. "We're not going to make this movie. Excuse me, gentlemen."

She straightened her spine and headed for the door. I had difficulty keeping up with her. I glanced back at the men in the conference room, their mouths hanging open in shock.

One of the men followed us to the outer office and asked, "Miss Turner, what should we do about the project?"

In a moment I can compare only with Joan Crawford's "Don't fuck with me, boys!" line to the board of directors at PepsiCo, Lana looked back and gave them her final comment.

"*Shelve* it!"

Lana and I posing at Le Dôme restaurant in Los Angeles circa 1980.
That evening was relaxed and mellow; one of our best together.

For My Truly 'God-given' Aug-82
and only Brother, Eric,
whose Love + Understanding
means everything in this
world To me! Just think
of all the other pleasures
we have yet To conquer—
With my Hearts Love,
Lana

P.S. Happy Birthday !!!

Lana was preparing for
an interview with *People*
magazine in 1982. She
softly said, "Hug me"
as the camera snapped
these poses of us.

Darling Eric —
Good morning!! — What
a crazy, frantic nite —
God will watch over
us, as He always does !!!
My Love always,
L—

above: Lana, her maid
Carmencita, and I
in 1984 as we arrived
at Los Angeles
International Airport.
I warned her, "Brace
yourself. Here come
the paparazzi."
left: Lana flashed a
gorgeous smile when
recognized at Los
Angeles International
Airport in 1984.

Sir Laurence Olivier knelt and kissed Lana's hand at the "Night of 100 Stars" in April 1985.

Photograph by Katia Beebe

Backstage at the "Night of 100 Stars" in 1985. Patti La Belle (center), was eager to meet Lana. Miss La Belle displays this photograph on the piano in her home.

A study in black and white at its most glamorous:
Lana and Raquel Welch with me at the "Night of 100 Stars" in
1985 when I first introduced them.

Lana always attracted paparazzi. This shot was taken in 1985 while she carried on a conversation with a persistent photographer. She asked him, "Do you have to keep taking pictures?" He answered, "You look stressed." Her quick retort: "Well, I'll look calm for you." He added, "Can you show me your nails?" Lana complied and whispered to me, "...That damn paparazzi..."

When I took this photo in 1972 at The Plaza Hotel in New York, it was four o'clock in the morning.

Lana loved having makeover shots taken through the years. *above:* Yiannis Karimalis did Lana's makeup for a stage play in Michigan. *left:* I gave her a makeover in 1972.

left: Lana was dressed in this beautiful white gown when we first met in 1971. *below:* Lana checks her look against a black backdrop.

This shot was taken in 1976. Lana's weight gain and her hair and makeup diminished her glamour.

Dearest Brother!
I forgot to pay you - last nite!
So - Here it is!!
and please come on Back
Home!!!
Love ya! -
Lil' Sis

Lana and I spent Christmas morning together in 1985. My gift to her was a framed scripture about love. She wore the bow from the wrapping in her hair.

left: This was backstage at The Tonight Show. Lana appeared on the show to promote her book, *Lana: The Lady, the Legend, the Truth. right:* Lana and I attended a signing for her book in Los Angeles in 1986.

Lana and I were out for the evening in New Orleans where she was performing in a play. She remarked, "I'm ready for jazz…"

Wed,

Darling Eric,
Good morning,
and Thank you
for our very good
talk last nite!
Remember "attitude"
is Positive, and
Healing! God will
guide and Protect
you! — Loved the
time with you, (all
too short) and love
you so dearly!!!
L.

This is one of the photos
Marilyn Monroe sent to
Lana in the early 1950s.
She inscribed, "I have al-
ways been a fan of yours....
I love your style; I love
your sophistication; and
I love your sex appeal.
Teach me those three..."

This photo was sent by Madonna to
Lana for her autograph. Lana signed
it "From one gutsy broad to another.
Lana." Madonna in turn sent Lana
a headshot of herself and signed it,
"Sincerely yours, Madonna." Lana
was taken aback by the lack of
warmth in Madonna's message.

Debbie Reynolds,
Lana, and I
together the night
the Thalians
honored Lana.
Terry Moore is
seen in the
background.

Three legendary divas; Lana, Ginger Rogers, and Lucille Ball, shot with my Instamatic camera backstage in 1985 at the "Night of 100 Stars." It took considerable convincing to get these talented women together for this shot.

This photo of Lana and June Allyson was shot in 1985 when I successfully brought them together once again after a long estrangement.

above: 1980 photo of Ginger Rogers, Lana, and me. *right:* In 1995 I visited Ginger Rogers at her home in Palm Springs and presented her with the photograph taken with Lana and me in 1980. She was thrilled that I had brought this memento to her and we became very dear friends.

Lana's gardener (far right), my sister Harriet (far left), and Lana's mother, Mildred Turner, (seated) at Lana's 1976 birthday celebration at her gardener's home in Malibu. I loved Lana's mother, Mildred Turner, like my own grandmother. We spent many good times together.

In 1979 Johnny Ray and I gave a surprise birthday party for Lana attended by her best friend, Virginia Grey (left).

Shown here are my sister Harriet, her son Peter, Virginia Grey, and Steve Bond, an actor on the soap opera, "General Hospital." Lana loved children, especially my nephew Peter. Here Lana is delighted with the birthday gift Peter gave her.

Lana's daughter, Cheryl, hosted Thanksgiving dinner in 1990. Lily Tomlin joined us for an evening of laughter and warmth.

Lana and I at her 1982 birthday party at my Pacific Palisades home.

We enjoyed a fun evening in 1985 at La Cage Aux Folles with Lana's daughter, Cheryl, (to the left of Lana) and Josh Leroy, Cheryl's girlfriend.

above left: Lana and I rode camelback together in Egypt in 1984. She did not enjoy the ride due to her intense fear of the animals. *above right:* This is another shot of us in Egypt safely on the ground where Lana was more relaxed. *left:* We were thrilled to meet Mrs. Anwar Sadat (left).

Lana and I visited an Egyptian temple before joining Robin Leach of *Lifestyles of the Rich and Famous* for a night of dancing on the Nile.

In Deauville, France in 1981 to attend the Lana Turner Film Festival a photographer admired our tans and asked to take this shot of us.

In Deauville, we posed in the Royal Hotel King's Suite. The enormous windows on the right offer a spectacular ocean view.

While dancing together at the Royal Hotel, Lana spotted Sean Connery seated at a table. She said, "Oh, there is Sean Connery. Discreetly turn your head and you'll see him. He probably feels guilty for not being friendly with me. Maybe he'll ask me to dance...." But he never did.

For Eric —
With Everlasting Faith
From your Everlasting
Loving Sis —
Lana

Lana gave me this spectacular photograph of herself.
It was taken fifty years ago. It remains my favorite shot of her
and is displayed in my bedroom.

~* 15 *~

Love Has Many Faces

THE EARLY YEARS

*W*hen Lana drank, she enjoyed telling stories about the men in her life: her husbands (seven) and her lovers (countless). She claimed to have lost her virginity to a young, handsome Beverly Hills celebrity attorney, Greg Bautzer, whose name is legendary in the bedrooms of Hollywood as well as in the divorce courts of Los Angeles County.

She stole her first husband, bandleader Artie Shaw, from two of her best girlfriends, Judy Garland and Betty Grable, both of whom were mad about the handsome clarinetist. Within the space of a year cracks began to appear in their marriage and divorce papers were filed. Between her divorce from Artie Shaw and her marriage to former actor Stephen Crane, Lana dated big-band leader Tommy Dorsey, singer Tony Martin, Dorsey's drummer Buddy Rich, and he-man actor Victor Mature (purloined from

Betty Grable who, in all fairness, gladly gave Lana his phone number).

She rarely discussed Stephen Crane with me except to say that, as with Artie Shaw, nothing between them seemed to be in sync. Lana and Stephen married on July 17, 1942 after which the two found out that his Juarez divorce from his wife had no validity in the United States. Now pregnant with her daughter, Cheryl, Lana's news sent Louis B. Mayer and the front-office executives in the "lion's den" at MGM into cardiac arrest. Lana, one of the studio's major stars, could ill afford to be involved in a scandal. Studios also had to contend with the censoring Hays Office and the morals clause I mentioned earlier. Will Hays, the czar of Hollywood morality, had more power at the time than Louis B. Mayer, and Mayer, like the other studio moguls, both respected and feared him.

Consequently, Mayer pulled the proper strings, had the marriage annulled, got the Mexican divorce sanctioned, and arranged a quickie remarriage to protect, first and foremost, the good name of MGM, followed by that of Lana Turner, and last (and probably least with Mayer), the unborn child.

The irony is that by the time she and Crane could lay claim to a legal marriage Lana no longer loved him. For the sake of her unborn child, MGM, and her career, she could not simply shed her soldier husband. With the country at war she was expected to be a good wife and keep the home fires burning.

Divorcing a man in the military was tantamount to treason. Hollywood had already come under the national microscope because so many leading men had found reasons to avoid military service.

After a respectable period of time and the birth of their daughter, they were quietly divorced. A free Lana once again went on the prowl.

In 1942 she'd had a flirtation with Robert Taylor while costarring with him in *Johnny Eager*. She admitted to me that she found him physically attractive—gorgeous, in fact—and that she was a big tease around him. Although Lana says they exchanged "passionate romantic kisses" both on and off the set, she denied they ever hit the sack together. Taylor, then married to Barbara Stanwyck, didn't dare get involved with the actresses in his films. Stanwyck planted spies on the sets of his pictures. Any untoward capers were promptly reported to the ever suspicious Mrs. Taylor, who always suspected the worst.

Years later Lana and Barbara were on some kind of publicity junket together. Quartered in the same hotel, Lana decided to make an effort to bridge the longstanding chasm between them. She picked up the phone and asked for Stanwyck's suite.

"Hello."

"Barbara, it's Lana. How are you?"

The kindest remark from Stanwyck was, "You goddam bitch!" followed by a string of expletives before she slammed down the receiver in Lana's ear. They never spoke again.

My father bore a remarkable resemblance to Robert Taylor and I recall Lana, in a conversation with my mother, commenting, "Anna, I can certainly see why you married him."

"And you're absolutely right, Lana," Mother said.

*A*fter the war ended, Lana's name became frequently linked in the press to handsome men about town—Rory Calhoun, Ricardo Montalban, Howard Hughes, and numerous others. Lana maintained she never entertained a serious interest in Howard Hughes, although she once told me that she found him likable. She considered his idiosyncracies quite odd, but his position of power helped her overcome some of her reservations. Lana also resented his appearance. Howard had already adopted a sloppy dress pattern, wearing the same dark gray slacks, a white shirt with missing buttons, and white tennis shoes sans socks. "At least," she assured me, "he bathed in those days."

Nevertheless, it did not thrill her when he showed up for a date unshaven, resembling more of a beach bum than one of the country's richest and most eligible bachelors. While she maintained she and Hughes were never intimate, they were obviously closer than casual acquaintances. One Hollywood rumor had it that they were briefly engaged for eight hours—an engagement that began on a coast-to-coast flight at takeoff and was called off before landing.

She never said anything to me about that trip or confirmed any engagement to Hughes. I know that she did fly with him because she confided to me, often gleefully, that Hughes enjoyed making sexual overtures in flight. Whether they ever played sexual games in the clouds, only the birds know for sure.

I do recall, though, that she couldn't bring up his name without discussing his passion for oral sex, "individually or both ways."

"You mean the sixty-nine position, Lana?" I queried.

"I think so."

In her autobiography she went into detail about his lust for oral sex. I'm inclined to take her word when she denied any sexual liaison with Howard. If nothing else, she was a young, beautiful actress with a healthy appetite for sex, and was an absolute neatness freak. That, in and of itself, may have contributed to the mutual attraction because Hughes, despite his disheveled appearance, had always been fearful of microbes and would place a Kleenex over a doorknob before placing his hand on it.

Lana expected her men to be right out of *Esquire* magazine. Hughes hardly fit the image.

Then there was the love of her life, the one she never denied: Tyrone Power, a man who used women to promote his own career. Yet it didn't prevent powerful leading ladies, who could have had their choice of handsome hunks, from losing their heads over him. Sonja Henie and Alice Faye quickly come to mind. Lana, no exception, kept his flame alive in her heart, which may be the reason she never quite made a success of her seven marriages.

"I loved him, Eric, in a way I never loved anyone else—*ever*! Both spiritually and emotionally, we had the ultimate connection. There was a lightning rod between us."

The most physical of her relationships, it was also the most intense. In those days the major studios controlled the lives of their stars. Louis B. Mayer boasted that there were more stars at MGM than there were in the heavens. He personally could take the credit for arranging more marriages and divorces than anyone else in the motion picture industry. He was a dictator to his contract players.

Mayer and 20th Century Fox's Darryl F. Zanuck, who had Power under contract, panicked over any romance between their two biggest moneymakers. Fans did not like their idols to be tied up in matrimony. Stars often kept their marriages secret from the public. Having children, especially for female stars, indicated growing older—a big taboo at the time.

Consequently, Louis B. Mayer kept Lana busy while Darryl Zanuck sent Tyrone on a European tour. A short time later, Lana, crestfallen, aborted their love child because, as she told me, "that's what Tyrone asked me to do." Power soon busied himself with sampling the European cuisine.

With Tyrone Power temporarily out of sight (at least to her thinking), Lana began dating Frank Sinatra with the sole purpose of making Tyrone jealous, hoping to lure him back into her arms. He didn't bite.

If Lana didn't conquer, she would often fall back on denial to save face. She dismissed any intimacy with Sinatra. Others on the scene disagreed, including his future wife, Ava Gardner, another of Lana's stablemates at MGM. In her 1990 biography, published posthumously, Ava wrote that Lana and Frank had "a very serious affair," and that Lana had been "deeply in love" with Sinatra, who supposedly had promised to divorce his first wife, Nancy, to marry Lana. Instead he married Ava.

Lana learned the news of Frank's betrayal from the morning paper over breakfast. "That son-of-a-bitch!" she said.

In the late fifties Sinatra repeated his treatment of Lana with a vulnerable Lauren Bacall, who was, at the time, coming to terms with the loss of her beloved husband, Humphrey Bogart, to the ravages of cancer. In her autobiography, *Lauren Bacall, By Myself*, she discusses her feelings about the relationship she had with Sinatra. Unlike Lana and other women, Bacall pulled no punches. She never, ever, forgave Frank, and never hesitates to say so.

It should also be noted that following World War II, Lana enjoyed a love affair with the handsome, exotic Turkish actor Turhan Bey.

I met Turhan Bey in 1994 near my home in Soboba Springs, California, adjacent to the San Jacinto mountains. I mentioned Lana and he recalled her with fondness. He was still devastatingly handsome. I couldn't wait to tell Lana, who had once told me she couldn't enjoy sex with him because his moustache distracted her.

"Lana," I asked, "why didn't you stay with him?"

"He was sought after by too many other women. Many beautiful starlets chased after him."

"He loved you," I said. "You were engaged, weren't you? Why didn't you get married? He would have married you in a minute."

Lana sighed. "It wouldn't have worked out. Like I said, he had his eyes on every woman in town."

"Would you like to see him again?"

She thought for a moment, sighed heavily and said, "Hmmm, sounds interesting," but her voice just trailed off.

My mother called Lana later and said, "I just met Turhan Bey. My son showed me some photos of him from the forties. God, but he's still so handsome. He's my age—seventy-three."

Lana surely winced when Mother gave his age.

It was about that time Lana was diagnosed with throat cancer. I could see she had made up her mind to be more reclusive. She did not want anyone to see how her looks might be slipping because of the disease.

Husband number three was New York socialite and sportsman Bob Topping, heir to a fortune of old money, which was controlled by his penny-pinching mother. But the family coffers, it had been rumored, were greatly diminished by Sonja Henie's divorce settlement from his brother Dan.

Topping aggressively pursued Lana with lavish gifts, particularly jewelry, which she loved. The heir to a supposed $100 million, he spent $25,000 on their engagement party, staged at the Mocambo night club, a popular celebrity hangout on the Sunset Strip in Hollywood. If held today, it would cost somewhere in the range of $150,000.

Topping had proposed to Lana at a New York watering hole called 21 by dropping a fifteen-carat marquis diamond in her martini glass. Ensuing presents included a two-inch-wide diamond bracelet then valued at $45,000.

Not known as a woman chaser, Topping had other expensive vices. His high-stakes gambling and excessive drinking, plus decreased access to the family vault, caused Lana to become the primary breadwinner in the marriage. One day, sitting at home with her mother and sipping a drink while going through a large stack of unpaid bills, she remarked, "I see a lot of money going out but very little coming in."

In a less-than-exaggerated response, her mother commented, "Let's face it, dear, you just can't afford to keep a millionaire." At first startled, Lana soon saw the humor and broke up in laughter.

Before her divorce from Topping became final, Lana, for the only time in her life, attempted suicide by slashing her wrists. The scars were red and ugly for a long time, so she began to wear broad bracelets in her films to conceal her failed attempt at self-destruction.

The bracelets served to hide her scars when she made *The Merry Widow* with hot new south-of-the-border leading man Fernando Lamas. No sooner could one say "Ole" than he and Lana were involved in a volcanic affair that rocked the production both on the set and in their respective dressing rooms.

Having met and conquered Lana, Lamas lost interest, definitely leaving her high and dry and disappointed. She had expected a proposal. She exacted her revenge by having him replaced by Ricardo Montalban as the male lead in her next film, *Latin Lovers*.

Although there has never been any overt hint that Lana and Montalban ever tangoed in the bedroom, throughout the years she maintained a high respect for him and his integrity. Twenty-three years later she personally selected Montalban to be her costar in *Madame X*, her last major Hollywood film.

Ironically, after *The Merry Widow*, Fernando Lamas proposed to and married actress Arlene Dahl, who, coincidentally, had recently divorced Hollywood's latest Tarzan—blond hunk Lex Barker. Stranger still, as strange things are wont to be in Hollywood, Tarzan would soon take Lana to be his new Jane.

During one of our many conversations in her twilight years, she told me that "Lex was physically the best lover I ever had. Not simply because he was well hung, which, my darling, he was, but because he was incredible at oral sex."

That came as no surprise to me. Throughout the many years of our relationship she'd told me many times that she preferred the oral route to conventional sex, "because," she would intimately whisper, "I was always *too tight*."

Lana absolutely detested Richard Burton, her leading man in the remake of her old flame Tyrone Power's big hit, *The Rains Came*, retitled *The Rains of Ranchipur*.

I recall that she'd once said something about Burton standing her up while they were making the picture. "He's nothing more than a whore master," she added.

"Why do you call him that?" I asked.

"Never mind. Just take my word for it."

Some years later Richard Burton gave me his story, thanks to the auspices of Valerie Douglas, Richard's adopted mother, agent-manager, and dearest friend, and also my dear friend and client for many years. I met Richard at Valerie's house, and while cutting his hair one day, I asked, "What really happened between you and Lana?"

He chuckled and, in that richest of all male voices, began the tale. "I arranged a dinner date with Lana after shooting one day and came to pick her up at the appointed time. Still in her dressing room, I assumed, getting ready. So I waited . . . and waited . . . and waited . . . and no Lana.

"Finally, I spied a young lady still working on the set and asked her if she would be kind enough to ask if Miss Turner would soon be coming out. She knocked several times on Lana's dressing-room door, but received no answer.

" 'Well,' I told her, 'I've been waiting for forty-five minutes. You're my witness. I'm only going to wait another fifteen minutes. If she doesn't come out, I'm leaving.' "

And he did.

Ten minutes after Burton departed, Lana stepped out of her dressing room, a vision of loveliness. "Where's Mr. Burton?" she asked the young woman.

"Miss Turner, Mr. Burton waited one hour and then he left."

"You mean to tell me he stood me up?"

"Miss Turner, he did not stand you up. He just decided to go."

"Bullshit! Fuck him! Tell the unit manager I'm not showing up on the set tomorrow."

The next morning one of the newspapers carried

a picture of Burton out nightclubbing with a lovely young starlet. Lana immediately called one of the film's producers and said she didn't want to work with Burton anymore.

In a fatherly manner the producer said, "Lana, you can't jeopardize the picture and your career over a personal clash of egos."

Burton continued the story. "The producer called me and presented his dilemma and asked if there wasn't some way we could iron things out. I acceded to his request. I am a professional. But relations between us were limited thereafter to lines of dialogue in the script."

When he finished, I reiterated Lana's brief response when I queried her. "She told me you stood her up."

Richard threw back his head and bellowed. "Fuck her! She can take her story to the grave. I didn't stand her up. It's not true. You just heard the truth!"

Valerie often asked me, "Eric, why do you put up with Lana? Why don't you stay away from that bitch?"

"I can't. She's not like that all of the time. Only when she's upset about something or been drinking does she take it out on me. Besides, she needs me."

Valerie's final comment on the subject was, "I wouldn't put up with it or stay with her if she paid me a million dollars."

No one seemed to understand. She needed me, and I loved her.

Of her latter-day husbands, Lana spoke only of the infamous, so-called Dr. Ronald Dante—her final excursion into matrimony.

"He was good in bed. Very good, in fact, but I felt an uneasiness in him that unnerved me. The vibrations were the worst," she said. "Besides, I married him on impulse. I did a lot of things in my life that I should not have done, on impulse. Marrying him was one!"

Ron Dante embezzled money from Lana. Shortly after they broke up, her Coldwater Canyon home was burglarized. More than $100,000 in uninsured jewelry was taken. The police tabbed it as looking like "an inside job."

In a rather obscure way, you might say I became one of the men in her life.

One evening in the mid-1980s, Lana and I were lying on her bed watching television. Quite unexpectedly we drifted into lovemaking as though it was just the natural thing to do. Lana, soft and loving, and I, somewhat tentative and tender. We explored each other like teenagers experimenting with first love.

The next morning when I got up I found this note pinned to my pillow: "Dear Eric—Good morning! What a sweet, crazy, funny night—God will watch over us—as he always does!!! My love always, L."

⨀ 16 ⨀

When Ladies Meet

*L*ana clearly preferred the company of men. She personified the old adage that "women do not like or trust other women." With the exception of her mother and daughter, she had few female friends.

During her early years at MGM, however, she ran with a group of young contract actresses that included Ann Rutherford, Betty Grable, Linda Darnell, and Virginia Grey. Virginia was one of the few women with whom Lana maintained a long-lasting, warm friendship. Eventually that friendship, too, would dissolve.

And there were others, not necessarily in her close circle, whom she genuinely admired. Of her costar in the 1941 production *Ziegfeld Girl*, Hedy Lamarr, Lana said, "She was the most beautiful creature I'd ever seen."

Judy Garland, also in *Ziegfeld Girl*, and Lana were friends from the time they first met at MGM in

1938, and remained close well into the fifties, although there were long lapses between contacts. Garland never pretended to be a raving beauty and found it humorous that anyone compared her with those gorgeous MGM women. Smart enough to know she couldn't compete with them in glamour, she didn't try. It is a tribute to her professionalism, humility, and talent that she never held personal grudges against the actresses themselves. Lana selected Judy to be her matron of honor when she married Stephen Crane.

Betty Grable, one of 20th Century Fox's money-making stars, and Lana shared the same taste in men (i.e., Artie Shaw and Victor Mature). Lana often joined Betty and actress Bonita Granville for lunch at Romanov's, dressed to the nines, giggling, gossiping, and attracting as much attention as possible.

Lana loved singer-actress Lena Horne, another MGM contract player. In 1975 Lana and I were in Chicago for her opening in *The Pleasure of His Company* at the Shubert Theater following Lena's one-woman show. We came into town early so Lana could do the usual unpacking, get her gowns hung up properly, and see to it that there were no last-minute glitches.

We went to see Lena's closing show. Backstage after her performance, these two gorgeous women embraced each other like long-lost sisters catching up on old times.

Lena said to me, ''I wish you could be with me to

do this," swirling one hand over her head to indicate her hair.

In the spirit of friendly rivalry Lana chuckled, "I'm keeping him with me."

I said, "Thank you, Lena. I'm flattered."

Whereupon Lena replied, "Why does everyone call me 'Leena'?"

"What do you mean?" I asked.

"Tell him, Lana."

"Honey, it's like when they call me 'Lana' instead of 'Lauhna,'" she said, pronouncing the former with the short "a" sound and the latter with the short "o" sound. "She wants to be called 'Lehna' Horne."

I had a great night with "Lauhna" and "Lehna."

Then Lana recalled a particular incident that took place when she and Lena were on an MGM promotional junket from Hollywood to New York on the Southern Pacific Railroad's *Super Chief*. Because of wartime restrictions and troop movements, sleeping accommodations were hard to come by. So these two megastars shared a compartment with separate beds. Lana was very careful that no one ever accused her of sleeping in the same bed with another woman.

Years later, her daughter Cheryl and Josh gave an interview to a lesbian magazine in which the writer alleges, "Before she passed away, Turner shared all kinds of stories with the couple, even explaining that she, too, was a lesbian."

Now it's my turn to say "Bullshit!" Lana Turner was the most *woman* I ever met. She loved men. She married seven of them.

Then there was Ava Gardner, also brought up at MGM and a longtime pal of Lana's. One of the most legendary stories out of Hollywood involved Ava, Lana, and Frank Sinatra. Everyone read the *Confidential Magazine* story about Sinatra busting in on Ava and Lana at Frank's place in Palm Springs. You can take your choice of the various versions of what happened. I know what Lana told me.

"Frank offered me and my manager, Ben Cole, the use of his Palm Springs home for a week. He and Ava were going through one of their many separations. Everyone knew Frank and Ava. Apart this week, together next week. We accepted them as they were.

"Ben and I were having a drink at Frank's bar when Ava and her sister unexpectedly arrived. The four of us were chatting comfortably and getting ready to have a bite to eat when, a short time later, Frank charged into the house like a raging bull and accused us of cutting him up. 'I bet you two broads have been getting off at my expense!' he said.

"Ava ignored him and went into the bedroom. Frank kept pace right behind her. I heard a lot of yelling, mostly foul language, and the sounds of breaking furniture and broken glass. Ben and I left without finishing our drinks."

Ava Gardner had a slightly different story to tell.

After an earlier argument with Frank in Hollywood, Frank told Ava, "I'm leaving, and if you want to know where I am, I'll be in Palm Springs fucking Lana Turner."

As he slammed the door on his way out, Ava called after him, "Fuck Minnie Mouse! See if I care!"

Ava, however, was never one to take such comments lightly. After having a couple of drinks to fortify herself, she picked up her sister, Bappie, around midnight and drove to Palm Springs, arriving at Frank's house sometime after two in the morning. Ava and Bappie sneaked around the house, peeping into windows and trying to see what was going on. When Lana and Ben discovered them, Lana called out, "Don't stand outside. You might catch something. Come on in."

They were all hungry and the four were about to sit down and eat some fried chicken. Before any of them took even one bite, Frank bounced into the house like a cyclone, filled with rage. From that point on Ava's story parallels Lana's. There are other versions, too. Among them, the most popular were:

(1) Frank caught Lana and Ava in bed together.
(2) Ava caught Frank and Lana in bed together.
(3) Frank caught Lana and Ava sharing his bed with another man.

The commotion brought out the Palm Springs police, along with flashing cameras and articles—

like you read in the *Confidential Magazine* version—accompanied by pictures, contrived or otherwise.

Lana swore to me that after she and Ben fled to find lodgings elsewhere, Ava's sister brought Ava to join them. Lana never wavered from the innocent scene of four people just having a good time. Just another Hollywood evening at home, "blown all out of proportion by those *rags*."

I know from Lana's irritation over Cheryl's public declaration of her lesbianism that she hated having private affairs smeared across the front pages of tabloids. As a star, she knew that no matter what happened to Cheryl, if it was something bad, it would be Lana Turner's name that would carry the story. Although she tried, she was unable to suppress anything so "juicy" as the Sinatra caper. I believe Lana told the truth.

Still, the rumors persisted. The most notorious was an underground story that had Ava Gardner, MGM's "raven-haired beauty," and Lana Turner, the studio's "most ravishing blond," picking up a gas jockey named Don and sharing his manly gifts when Sinatra came upon the scene. When reprimanded by a member of the MGM brass, Ava reportedly cooed in her sultriest I-just-got-back-from-Nawth-Carolina whisper, "Don't worry, honey, who'd believe it?"

Lana and Ava were personal friends and kept in touch frequently, but there is no hard-core proof of anything lurid between them. I was with Lana one day when she picked up the phone and put in a call to Ava at her London flat. Ava told Lana, "I just saw your picture in the paper. You look fantastic. Your hair looks incredible."

"Here," Lana said with a flicker of pure mischief in her eyes, "talk to the creator."

She handed me the receiver and I was stuck, for one of the few times in my life, without words. Not for long, however. Who could resist the glamorous, sultry-voiced Southern siren from MGM?

In 1990, when a friend called me and said he'd read in the papers that Ava was quite ill and probably dying, I immediately relayed the news to Lana. Lana again dialed Ava's London number directly and was told by someone in attendance that "Miss Gardner is unavailable, Miss Turner."

Lana left a brief message and her telephone number. Ava never returned the call. Three to four months later the headlines heralded her glamorous life and death. Lana became quite depressed. Another MGM legend had passed into history. Who would be next? It never occurred to Lana that she was even on the list.

Because they were both from the South, Lena Horne was a much closer friend to Ava than to Lana. In Ava's autobiography, Lena Horne was asked to contribute a chapter. In it she wrote: "Ava Gardner had great inner warmth that, for instance, I never saw in Lana. She was way down. She was Ava, not Ava Gardner the star. I don't think Ava thought about it that way."

A more diplomatic Ava wrote, "I really liked Lana. She was a nice girl and she felt neither anger nor malice toward Frank and me," referring to Sinatra's earlier walkout on Lana when he returned to his wife, ending their affair.

Lana liked Elizabeth Taylor, whom she'd known as a child, but always refused invitations to holiday functions or dinner parties at Elizabeth's house once she became the wife of Richard Burton. Her loathing of Burton was absolute.

She enjoyed Debbie Reynolds but considered her to be too hyper and frantic. She respected Debbie's efforts to involve her in the Thalians and other Hollywood causes.

Lana well understood and respected Bette Davis's place in the Hollywood firmament. Just as there was only one Lana Turner, she knew there sure as hell was no other Bette Davis. Lana never lacked savvy when it came to stardom.

In 1989 she and Davis spoke on the phone. Bette knew Lana had been the 1981 guest of honor at the Deauville Film Festival, to which she had just been invited in the same capacity. Despite a recent series of debilitating illnesses and strokes, Bette had managed to complete a feature film with Ann Sothern and the absolutely indestructible Lillian Gish called *The Whales of August*. She was determined to keep her image alive on the talk shows and late-night TV circuits.

Just prior to her departure for Deauville, Bette

called again and asked Lana for advice. She knew that Lana's daughter, just like her own daughter, B.D., had written an unflattering book about her mother. She publicly railed against B.D.'s book and undoubtedly shared Lana's horror on the publication of Cheryl's book.

At Deauville Miss Davis suffered the final indignities of stroke and the ravages of time. Monuments crumble slowly, but they do crumble.

Speaking of sadness, Lana's longtime wonderful friendship with Virginia Grey (which began in the thirties at a time when Bette Davis busied herself teaching Hollywood about the iron will of women) ended on a bitter note when Lana, on advice of her doctor, had to give up the bottle.

She and Virginia were on the phone one day. "Lana," she said, "we need to get together and have a drink."

Lana said, "Maybe you didn't hear me, Virginia. I said I am not drinking anymore." They never spoke again. That's how Lana did it. When she cut the cord, it stayed cut.

Lana had nurtured and protected Virginia over the years by insisting she be used in her films, particularly in the Ross Hunter productions. Hunter had begun to refer to Virginia as "my good-luck charm."

Although they never spoke again, Lana's loyalty remained steadfast.

✒ 17 ✒

The Empress Instructs the Ingenue

*M*arilyn Monroe grew up a fan of Lana Turner. In a strong way, she loved Lana. She considered Lana to be a "goddess." I know this from both Lana and Dorothy Davis, one of Marilyn's best friends, who came to Hollywood with Betty Grable, and who is now my dear friend.

I have two very precious, rare photos that Marilyn sent Lana with the message, "Please, *please* sign these for me and send them to me. Your signature will be immortalized in my heart."

Lana never did. Instead, she said, "I will talk to you on the phone. We will meet and I will teach you how to walk, how to act, what to say, and what not to say."

When they got together, Lana, tough and businesslike, cut right to the chase. "You've got to change your makeup. You've got to get rid of some of those bulges you have. Everything must change."

There can be no doubt that Lana had a tremendous influence on Marilyn Monroe at the beginning of her acting career—and Stanislavsky can choke on that. In a city where it is said there are no secrets, this one has been kept for posterity, and this, my friends, is posterity!

Lana knew, going in, that Marilyn Monroe would be a lasting element in the jigsaw puzzle of moviedom. In the beginning, I'm sure, she didn't realize just how lasting Monroe's career might be, but Lana had a keen eye for talent that could be developed. She felt Monroe had the makings. Her only doubts were whether or not Marilyn would accept her destiny and become the professional she was capable of being.

Marilyn and Lana were attracted to each other on a friendship level. At that time Lana's schedule left little room for anything outside her own career. Busy making films, often more than one at a time, she traveled extensively from country to country, building her own image. She didn't have time to personally train Marilyn on a daily basis, but she hoped to be able to help mold the young starlet into what she might become—a dramatic actress.

Instead, Marilyn turned out to be an international sex symbol, but she made her mark. She created the age of the sexpot. Lana, on the other hand, had the sophistication of a socialite. She might have come from the blue book of American high society.

She certainly would have blended in with that lofty element.

Lana, in the context of her youth, could also be considered a sexpot. The difference, however, had to do with the era in which such women were sprung upon the American psyche. Where Lana's sweater caused men to pant in the thirties, Marilyn's low-cut blouses aroused the same male hormones in the fifties.

Marilyn was told by her mentors, "You do it this way." She obeyed. For her, it worked. However, she almost created a firestorm when she told her agent, her producers, her directors, and the casting people that "Lana told me to wear it this way."

"Lana who?" they would ask. "Oh, are you friends with Lana Turner?"

Catching her slip, Marilyn would respond in the demure voice that made her famous, "Oh, no. My friend Lana from Idaho."

She would repeat these stories to Lana, who thought they were just hilarious. Lana would later relate them to me.

I said, "Lana, do you know what this means? You were a phone pal of Marilyn Monroe's."

She said, "Honey, shut up. I am already a celebrity. I don't need to be glorified by the name of another star."

"Ah, but you are admitting she was another 'star,' Lana."

"Did I?"

"You've talked about Mamie Van Doren and Jayne Mansfield and Diana Dors, and you know it."

"Those broads tried to copy me."

"But, darling," I told her, "all of you have different personalities."

She said, "Bullshit! They all have the same toner in their hair like I do and the same bleach and they *all* want to dress like I do. You know what?"

"What?"

"There's only one Lana Turner—and it's *moi*."

I thought to myself, *Wow! That's an egotistical, self-centered statement.*

Lana felt, from the beginning, deep in her heart, that Marilyn Monroe would become a well-known "symbol," a monument for the rest of her life. She told this to Marilyn, who responded with the question, "Why do you say that?"

Lana once told me, "You know what, Eric? She was such a dumb broad when she came to Hollywood, but there was something about her heart and her mind that I cared for."

When Marilyn's career became an established fact, Lana didn't hear from her so often.

Once, when Lana was in the process of moving and we were going through things to keep and things to get rid of, I ran into a couple of photographs. Holding the pictures up, I asked, "Who is this?"

Lana glanced at them and said, "Oh, darling, please, don't give me that who-is-this shit."

"Lana," I said, looking straight into her face, "Baby, I'm not playing around. Who is this? She's beautiful."

"That's Marilyn Monroe."

I remembered the story she'd told me before. "What are you doing with these pictures?"

She shrugged.

I said, "Oh my God, she was so beautiful, so cute."

When she sent the photographs to Lana to autograph, she sent along a letter saying, "I just had my hair bleached and I'm not sure if I like it. My hair is kind of damaged. Do you like it?"

Lana said, "Eric, this woman's whole personality changed when she changed the color of her hair to blond." She turned and asked, "Do you want these photos, darling?"

"Yes," I quickly answered, before she changed her mind.

"You mean," she quickly pounced, "you're more of a fan of hers than you are of me?"

I said, "Baby, you're my family. I didn't know Marilyn."

"Okay, here, take these things. I don't want them."

I grabbed them. She'd had a few drinks. I'm sure she later regretted giving them to me, but I kept them.

That's the story. Generational sex symbols.

⚞ 18 ⚟

Egypt—Another
Time, Another Place

*I*n 1984 Robin Leach invited Lana to be his special guest in a two-part episode of "Lifestyles of the
Rich and Famous." She agreed to go only if I accompanied her. Leach readily agreed and granted her
other accommodation requests, including first-class
hotel for two, first-class airfare for two, around-the-
clock transportation, and the full star treatment.
Lana may not have graced the silver screen in recent
years but she still remained, as Louella Parsons always said, "a real movie star." People deferred to
her stardom because she demanded it.

We were checked into a lavish suite of rooms at
the New Cairo Marriott Hotel, an 1869 Egyptian
palace in the process of being extensively refur-
bished. From within our sumptuous suite I fanta-
sized Cleopatra and Marc Antony enjoying such
luxury.

After settling in for the evening, I awakened from

a sound sleep itching and scratching. I reached over, pulled the light chain, threw off the bed covers, and was confronted with what looked like a caravan of Egyptian ants crossing the Sahara (later determined to be a caravan of Egyptian cockroaches). Expecting cobras in a basket any second, I let out a yelp that could be heard in the lobby several floors below us.

Grabbing a towel and tossing it around my torso, I ran into Lana's bedroom, where she was propped up in bed watching Egyptian television, not understanding a single word they said. I remember her once saying, "Good acting doesn't need dialogue."

"Lana!"

She looked up, startled as if I'd jumped out of the picture tube, a question poised on her face, but no words.

"Lana! We have some strange bugs, and they're in a long line."

"You're just being melodramatic."

"Oh? Well, come on into my bedroom and see for yourself."

Clad in a very unglamorous housecoat, she got out of her own bed and allowed me to lead her by the arm to see the invading army. She leaned over my bed to see for herself.

"Those sons of bitches!"

It had taken us five hours just to hang up her wardrobe and put away her booze and jewels. She referred to this lengthy procedure as "setting up housekeeping."

She said, "Excuse me, brother. I'm making a phone call to the management. Now!" And she did.

The manager and his entourage were in our suite within thirty seconds. Lana confronted the perplexed manager head-on, pointing to our little welcoming committee. "What the hell is this?" she demanded.

"What," he asked, "is what, Miss Turner?"

"Put your glasses on."

He looked down closely and said, "Oh, Miss Turner, the people who occupied this suite before were a family of seven nomads from Saudi Arabia. We've *never* entertained insects."

"I don't give a shit," she said, "if they were nomads from China."

"Miss Turner," he almost begged, "what can we do for you?"

"I need assistance, and so does my brother, to pack and get the hell out of here. We are leaving!"

Attempting to pacify the angry screen siren in a housecoat, he proffered, "Please, Miss Turner, before you make that decision, let me offer you the presidential suite—our most lavish accommodations—compliments of the management."

Lana looked at me, eyes flashing fire, and then at him and said, "I don't understand why you didn't give us that suite in the first place." She turned to me and asked very sternly, "Brother, do you want to look at this other suite?"

"Let's do it," I said.

We were escorted up to the presidential suite. The big double doors swung open. My natural reaction was "Ahhh."

Lana, ever the star, demanded, "Where are the beds?"

They took us to my bedroom first. She said, "Step aside," and grabbed the corner of the covers, sweeping them away from the bed. She put on her "reading glasses," dug into her purse for a magnifying glass, and then, motioning toward some chairs, instructed everyone to "please be seated." Five Egyptian men, totally awestruck at this tempestuous performance, politely obeyed her command.

Leaning over until her nose almost touched the bed, she checked the tops of the sheets, the pillows, under the pillows, and then proceeded to rip the sheet off the mattress. When she finished in my bedroom we all moved, like toy soldiers, into her master bedroom, where she performed the same inspection.

Once the suite had the Turner Good Housekeeping Seal of Approval (at two in the morning), the manager said, "Miss Turner, you probably have an early call—why don't you get some rest and my staff will transfer your belongings to this suite."

"Thank you, no. I don't want all of those—whatever you call them—*insects*—in our wardrobe."

The manager assured her that the only things to be transferred were her possessions—not the uninvited guests. Only then did she agree. She still insisted on personally checking each item as it was brought into the suite. She had a fetish about anyone going through her personal belongings except herself, her maid, and myself.

By five-thirty in the morning, exhausted, we both fell into bed. I woke up around ten, Lana shortly after twelve. We had an appointment with Robin Leach at one o'clock. Impossible! Lana Turner couldn't be ready for anyone in an hour's time—and face cameras? Forget it.

Robin phoned our suite to let us know he was on his way and the cameras were awaiting us at the Cairo Museum. I relayed Robin's message to Lana.

Lana replied, "I don't give a shit. Nobody rushes me. I'll cancel this whole thing, pay for the trip myself. We'll enjoy Egypt for a couple of days and go home."

It didn't matter to Lana that the film crew had to be considered, as well as the extensive preparations—and, more importantly, the value of the show at this point in her life. It mattered to me. I had to protect her from herself, something I found myself doing on a more frequent basis.

Once again, the task of compromise and making peace fell to me. Robin waited for her answer. I went back to the phone. "Robin, she is not ready." I explained the turmoil that went on the night before.

"Eric," he said, "do me a favor. I'll be over at two o'clock instead of one. We'll just sit in the living room of your suite and wait as you do whatever it is you have to do to get her ready.''

Lucky me. Lana, like most beautiful women I've known, seemed always to sense being rushed if time became an issue. In such instances she would take more time. It was not unusual for her to use this ploy as an excuse to cancel out. I've spoken to other people associated with stars, and there is a common thread among them. Marilyn Monroe, Jayne Mansfield—they all ''borrowed'' time for themselves.

Robin arrived with his secretary and waited in the living room. He waited and waited. I knocked on Lana's door and she said, ''Yes?''

''Darling, they're here.''

''Who is here?''

''Robin and his secretary.''

''Come on in,'' she said to me, her tone quite nasty. She hadn't done her makeup. I still had to do her hair. It was two o'clock. ''Why did you let them in?'' she snapped.

Instead of screaming at her, I used reverse psychology, which always worked. ''Sweetheart, we've come all this way and I've been looking forward so much to seeing the museum.'' I hugged her. I could feel her shaking, which she usually did when rushed. I held her until she stopped shaking.

She looked at me and said, ''Darling, tell them I'll be out as soon as possible.''

I left her and entertained Robin and his secretary. The three of us waited together. At four-thirty the bedroom door opened and out came Lana Turner, glamour queen.

For the second day Robin had arranged a variety of locations in front of major Egyptian monuments. Because of her previous day's tardiness, we were only half an hour late. It came as a shock, however, that Robin wanted us both seated astride camels moving across the landscape in front of the Sphinx and the Great Pyramids. Talk about nomads in the desert.

Lana took one look at the tall beast and froze, scared shitless. In an effort to be a good sport, she prepared to "mount" the camel when, without any warning, the beast—unpredictable as camels are known to be—turned and spat all over her clean white linen slacks. She intended to wear black slacks, but when she saw that I wore white, she changed her mind. She said, "Darling, we must be coordinated."

A less fastidious star would have simply gone on with the scene, but not Lana Turner. She insisted on having the limo drive us back to our hotel, where she changed into a fresh pair of white slacks and threw the soiled ones into the wastebasket. The limo returned us to the location as if nothing had happened. The production company didn't lose much, "only an hour," Lana cooed.

Our trials and tribulations with the camel had only just begun. Lana came close to being thrown on several occasions when she tried to navigate the dromedary across the sand and boulders. Her look of horror as the camel reared up and took off in a gallop is etched into the video.

Whenever the camel humped, Lana threw her legs up toward its neck and yelled, "Oopah! Oopah!" Hysterical with laughter, I'd never seen such a performance in my life. I kept thinking, *I'm going to lose my little sister.* I couldn't imagine anything so gauche as dying on "Lifestyles of the Rich and Famous." It would have been a first for Robin Leach.

After the shoot, with both Lana and myself back on terra firma, she said to Robin, "I would like to spend two or three hours with my brother, alone."

The two of us walked up a slight incline, overlooking the Sphinx. At the top of the knoll she touched my arm and said, "Stop." Looking at me, she said, "Darling, I have been here before with you."

Later, at a different shoot, while walking through an Egyptian bazaar, Lana wanted to discuss her newfound feelings of reincarnation, much to the delight of Robin Leach. She described the magical powers of the Scarab which warded off evil.

A major scenario of the program took place aboard the *Nile Pharaoh*, an Egyptian riverboat for tourists who wish to see Egypt from the river, not too far removed from Cleopatra on her barge. Lana insisted on taking this cruise.

The day was bright and wonderful and sunny when we boarded the boat. The captain had a special surprise in store for Lana. Unbeknownst to either of us, he had arranged for Mrs. Anwar Sadat, the former First Lady of Egypt, her daughter, and several bodyguards to take this trip down the Nile with us.

The captain lent me a video camera and even arranged for some romantic music. Lana and I enjoyed it so much we asked if we could borrow the tape. The request so pleased him that he asked Lana to accept it as his humble gift. It was a day of perfection. Lana, relaxed and happy, never looked more radiant and glamorous. She didn't need evening gowns to look glamorous; she naturally radiated glamour. Remember, she came to stardom in a sweater.

When I went to the upper level of the boat I saw, out of the corner of my eye, someone who seemed familiar but I couldn't place the face. As several bodyguards surrounded the woman, I realized, "Oh my God—it's Mrs. Sadat."

I approached slowly, ever aware of the bodyguards and their pistols at the ready. Almost in slow motion, I softly said, "Good morning, Mrs. Sadat." She seemed to already know me. "I'm Eric Root from . . ."

Before I could finish, she gave me a lovely smile and said, as if I were an old friend, "My dear, how are you? You have come to Egypt with my husband's favorite actress."

I said, "Mrs. Sadat, that actress is on the level below us. She would be so honored to meet you."

"No, my dear, don't disturb her on this beautiful

trip down the Nile. I wouldn't interrupt her at this point."

"But, Mrs. Sadat, Lana would consider it a great privilege to meet you. I'm going down right this minute to tell her you are here. I'm sure she will be ecstatic."

I returned to the lower deck, went over to Lana's chair, and said, "Darling, you'll never guess who is on the deck above us."

Failing to grasp my excitement, she remained composed. "Who did you see, dear?"

I leaned down to Lana and in a low and subtle voice said, "Mrs. Sadat."

Lana gasped, suddenly animated and excited. "Darling, you know how much I've always wanted to meet them."

"Lana, it's just Mrs. Sadat. You remember, her husband was assassinated."

"Oh yes. How sad."

I told Lana I'd make an effort to bring Mrs. Sadat down to meet her. Lana spoke sharply. "No, darling, no. Thank you, but you will escort me upstairs to meet her."

We linked arms and proceeded up the stairway. What a delightful scene: bringing two such vibrant and exciting women together while cruising the Nile.

I introduced Lana to Mrs. Sadat. The former First Lady said in a soft and warm voice, "I humbly say to you, Miss Turner, that I am honored to meet you at last. My late husband was one of your greatest fans, as am I.''

Lana stared at this gracious lady, who had endured so much pain and suffering, then removed her oversized sunglasses and said to Mrs. Sadat, ''I have a tear,'' just as one, indeed, trickled down her cheek.

The two embraced each other as if they were old friends being reunited. The delighted photographers' shutters clicked. Until the end of her days, Lana considered this one of her great life experiences.

On the day we left Egypt to fly back to Hollywood, stopping for a brief visit in New York, we ''got ourselves together.'' Everything was put in order: passports, gifts, newspapers all hastily stuffed into our carry-on luggage as the bellboys put her heavier luggage on the trolley.

Unlike some travelers who place comfort above all else, Lana insisted that while we could be informal, we must always be well groomed and presentable. We never traveled in sweats and Nikes, like so many of the nouveau stars.

Lana insisted I wear blazers and Ivy League ties. Only when the sun was blazing hot, as on this occasion, would she say to me in a condescending tone, ''Darling, today you don't have to wear a tie.''

Finally, we stepped into the long corridor leading to the lobby exit where our limousine awaited us.

Wherever and whenever I escorted Lana, her eyes were always fixed straight ahead as though she had tunnel vision. She did not saunter. She strode, erect, eyes forward, always the professional, never into small talk. She took deliberate steps as she crossed the lobby while guests and employees craned to get one last glimpse of the blond American movie star.

I hoped she would grace the people standing around with at least a wee smile, but she stared dead ahead, like a horse with blinders. Those people didn't exist. Her focus remained on the limousine awaiting our arrival. I, however, frequently turned and smiled at people. I often wondered if they thought me a star, too.

As we exited the foyer I noticed a gentleman surrounded by a gaggle of children, an absolutely gorgeous man, perhaps six-foot-five, dressed magnificently in a long white tunic. He strongly resembled Omar Sharif, the fabulous Egyptian hunk.

I whispered, "Lana, look back. Please look back."

"Who is it?" she asked, stubbornly resisting the intrusion.

I growled, "Shit! Stop right now. Turn around and let him see you. I *know* this man is following us. He is mesmerized. I know. Do as I ask. Just turn around and see for yourself. Shake hands with him. Take him by surprise and say, 'How do you do, I'm Lana Turner.'"

Fiercely, she snapped at me, "I would *never* do that."

I tried again. "Lana, he's wealthy. He's handsome. He's probably a prince. He could be your next husband."

Her sidelong glance said, "Don't be an asshole."

We arrived at the limo. The driver jumped to attention, opened the door, and we stepped inside. The tinted window went up and Lana instructed the chauffeur, "Drive on!"

"Don't drive off," I countermanded.

Lana's look should have withered me, but it didn't. I tried one more time. "Lana, this could be the love of your life, darling. Just give him one little moment. I'll never coax you again, I promise."

"Okay. Okay. What do you want me to do?" she wearily sighed in exasperation.

Outside the limo the gentleman stood at the curb, a few feet away from us. I frantically attempted to push the button to open the window, but it wouldn't work for me. The chauffeur, sensing my frustration, released the lock and the window glass disappeared into the door. The handsome stranger approached, leaned into the back seat, and stared at us with piercing black eyes.

He said, ever so romantically, "You are so beautiful."

Lana looked up at him sweetly and, in a voice like melted honey, responded, "Thank you so much."

He seemed confused. "No, no, Madame—*him*!" he said, pointing his forefinger toward me. He handed his card to Lana and said, "Will you please give this to him?"

"Like hell I will."

I reached across her, took the gentleman's card,

and put it in my pocket. I met him again—many years later. He had five wives, heaven only knows how many "boys," and, yes, he *was* a real prince.

Lana thought it was a big hoot by the time we were aboard the plane and she'd had a couple of drinks. We both had a good laugh.

In the aftermath of our Egyptian experience, Lana spoke less and less of religion and gravitated more toward metaphysics. Reincarnation became uppermost in her beliefs. Through her books, Shirley MacLaine became sort of a guru to Lana. Analysis of Shirley's theories gradually replaced our biblical discussions.

⊰ 19 ⊱

Night of a Hundred Stars

*W*e didn't know it then, but Lana's appearance on the fabled "Night of a Hundred Stars," at Radio City Music Hall in New York City, would mark the occasion of her last great public appearance. Put together by the celebrated theatrical producer Alexander Cohen, it promised to be the gala to end all galas. Lana, excited about being invited, said to me, "Darling, there will be legends there who were legends long before me."

Plans for televising this event involved a week of stressful preparation, rehearsals, cocktail parties, and receptions. A suite at the Plaza Hotel had been reserved for us.

On one particular evening prior to the big event, there was a reception for the numerous celebrities in attendance, many of whom had never previously met. Lana looked spectacular—it truly was her last hurrah. I must preface this particular evening by saying that, several years earlier, I had accompanied Richard Burton and Valerie Douglas to the opening of an Italian restaurant on Pico Boulevard in Los Angeles. Lana, as she all too often did, canceled out at the last minute, either because Burton would be there or for reasons of personal insecurity.

I went alone and enjoyed myself immensely. One of the highlights for me that evening had been meeting Raquel Welch and her daughter, Tahnee. I chatted with Tahnee and liked her immediately. She told me, "Mama really likes you, Eric."

I soon found myself engaged in a lengthy conversation with the stunning Raquel Welch. Richard, as always, was in rare form, and we had a grand evening.

On the "Night of a Hundred Stars" Lana, dressed in white, was a vision in platinum, her hair in champagne and platinum tones, her form dripping in diamonds and wrapped in white mink.

As we walked in I caught sight of Raquel sitting alone, equally dramatic in black. I said to Lana, "Excuse me, darling, I must go over and say hello to Raquel."

Raquel said, "Eric, how nice to see you. How have you been?"

"Just fine, Raquel. By the way, you know who I'm with this evening."

"Of course. You're with Lana. Did you know, we've never met?"

"I didn't know that."

"As a kid growing up I always loved her movies, and I've always wanted to meet her."

I went back to Lana, now engaged in conversation with someone I'd never met. I politely intruded and said, "Lana, when you're through, I'll be in the ballroom with Raquel, and she would love to meet you."

Lana replied, "I'd like to meet her, too."

A flash of light hit me. Lana's all in white. Raquel's all in black. What a stunning picture. I knew I'd have to present the idea to Lana with kid gloves. I approached her with caution after she agreed to come and meet Raquel.

"Lana, I have a photographer who wants a picture of the three of us together."

She raised an eyebrow. "The three of us?"

"Yes. Would that be okay? It's a wonderful concept. You're in white, she's in black, and it would make a fantastic picture."

Knowing Lana's ego (incidentally, she always denied having a movie star ego; it was always "a healthy ego"), I knew the only way she'd agree to pose with another beautiful superstar, especially a younger one, would be to couch it in terms of how dramatic and historical it would be.

"Can't you see it?" I asked. "You'll be perfect opposites. How about it? Can't we take the photo of the three of us?"

She mulled the dramatic possibilities and finally consented. "Yes, that would be okay."

I introduced the two film stars, from separate generations—which I diplomatically failed to mention—and they chatted idly while the photographer prepared his camera. The resulting picture, as stunning as I had hoped, became an all-time favorite.

An even more spectacular photo opportunity lurked just around the corner. Over the years I'd met Laurence Olivier on numerous occasions in Hollywood. He always remembered me as that "tall blond young man." I saw him at the reception and went over to say hello.

"Mr. Olivier, how are you?"

"Eric, my boy, fine, thank you, and yourself?"

"Great. I'm here with—"

"I see who you are with. How is that beautiful child?"

"Wonderful. Of course you know that she is a total fan of yours."

Sir Laurence remarked, "I don't know if you are aware that we have never met."

"Really?" I was genuinely surprised, because they were contemporaries and Lana rarely missed the opportunity to meet a man as handsome as Olivier had been as a young man. She'd told me many times how much she stood in awe of his talent. "Maybe I can rectify that omission. May I bring her over to meet you?"

"No, I'll go over to her."

I knew he wasn't well, so I persuaded him to allow me to bring Lana to his table.

I returned to Lana, now deep in conversation with Robert Wagner, Jill St. John, Vic Damone, and Diahann Carroll.

"Excuse me," I interrupted, "Lana, guess who wants to meet you?"

"Who, dear?"

"Sir Laurence Olivier!"

"No!" she exclaimed, placing her bejeweled hands up to her face. "Give me a few minutes to digest this."

On my way to the men's room I spotted a photographer. I asked him if he could take what I thought would be a very important picture.

"No," he replied brusquely. "I'm on special assignment. A picture of who?"

"Laurence Olivier being introduced by me to Lana Turner."

"I don't think so," he said.

I couldn't believe it. Lana Turner meeting Sir Laurence? Was this man stupid or something? "But can't you see what a coup it is?"

Unimpressed, he said, "No, I have other assignments."

Five minutes passed, during which I frantically searched the room for a photographer to record history in the making. Finally I spotted a lady with a camera wearing a *Life* magazine press badge.

"Pardon me," I said. "Could I speak to you for a minute?" I revealed my plan to her. At first she said no, but when I explained what I wanted, she agreed.

Her name was Katia Beebe. I brought her and her camera with me to first meet Lana, and then the three of us approached the Olivier table.

Lana said, "I've watched so many of your movies. They've always had such meaning. I'm so nervous."

He did not rise, but looked up into Lana's eyes and said, "My sweet beauty, I am honored to meet you." He pushed back his chair, knelt on one knee and kissed her, as a gentleman would, softly on her left hand.

SNAP! Katia Beebe recorded the moment for posterity. Within days the photograph, which no one seemed to want to take, ran as a full-page picture in *Life* magazine beneath the simple caption, "Just one more . . ."

Today, Katia Beebe is a successful film producer living in Beverly Hills and a dear friend of mine. Her partner Ron Schneider is my manager.

It became Lana's last great still shot, a shot flashed around the world.

We'd had a perfect evening. What a pity it would be marred by one unfortunate incident. Lana did not like escalators. She feared one of her heels getting caught between the steps. As we left the reception and stepped onto the down escalator, her worst nightmare became reality. One of her heels wedged between two steps. As she fell forward I reached out and caught her just in time to avoid a real disaster.

There was no dearth of photographers this time.

The paparazzi managed to fully cover her fall and, without asking what happened, all of the New York papers carried pictures with various captions, insinuating that Lana might be under the influence. Ironically, this time she really was innocent.

The week presented many amazing photographs. The night after Sir Laurence, Raquel, the escalator, and tabloid press, and prior to the taping of the show, Lana and several film legends were waiting backstage for their calls. Lana, who never liked me brandishing my camera at such dignified affairs, displayed shock this time that I didn't bring one, because she knew this night would not be ordinary. She surprised me by reaching into her purse and retrieving her own camera, which she handed to me. "Just in case," she smiled slyly.

Within a few moments I spotted Lucille Ball without her husband, Gary Morton, sitting in a chair, also waiting. Lucy motioned me over to her. "I just want you to know you're a very striking man and the fact that you're with Lana is interesting because you make a very striking pair," Lucy said. Looking at Lana's hands, she asked, "Who does her nails?"

"My sister Harriet. She comes to Lana and does them every couple of weeks."

Lucy reached into her purse, took out a scrap of paper, quickly scribbled her phone number, and handed it to me. "Could you have her give me a call? I'd love to have my nails look like that."

(When I later told Lana, she became furious and

instructed me never to give Lucille Ball or anyone else my sister's number, thereby cutting off any opportunity for major new clients.)

"Thank you, Miss Ball."

"Call me Lucille." Lucille looked in Lana's direction and asked, "Won't your lady be missing you?"

"She's busy."

"What's that in your hand?"

"A camera." I almost blurted out that it was Lana's camera, but caught myself. I noticed Ginger Rogers, also waiting nearby, which gave me another of my bright ideas.

"You know, Lucille," I chose my words carefully, "what a picture it would be—you, Ginger, and Lana together—legends in their own time."

She responded with a short but sweet no.

"But really. Think about it. Incredible!"

"You seem like a nice guy. Okay, but you better ask Ginger first. I know Lana would do it, but I don't know about Ginger. We are not close and have absolutely nothing in common. We never did." She paused while I digested her words, then she added, "But if you can get her to go along with it, it's okay with me."

"Thank you, Lucille. I'll see what I can do."

I then approached Ginger, camera in hand. "Miss Rogers?"

"Yes."

"My friend Lana and my new friend Lucille have agreed to allow me to take a picture of the three of you together. Would you be so kind as to allow me that favor?''

''Absolutely not!''

I turned to leave, having been rejected, then turned back and tried again. ''Please, Miss Rogers, just a quick shot of the three of you.''

''Oh, all right, but let's get it over with—and remember, I'm doing this because Lana is a sweet kid, *not* for Lucille.''

I never moved so fast in my life. I rushed back to Lucy and said, ''Ginger has agreed.''

''Oh, fuck!'' Lucy muttered under her breath. ''Hurry up and put us where you want us. Let's get the damned thing over.''

I trotted back to Ginger. ''Could you sit over there, Miss Rogers?'' I said, pointing toward Lucy.

''What? Okay. Hurry,'' she added.

Taking a seat near Lucy she rather formally said, ''Hello, Lucille, how are you?''

''Fine, Ginger, baby, how the hell are you? We haven't talked for years.''

I left them together and dashed to get Lana. ''Lana,'' I almost gushed, ''look over there in the corner.'' I was as proud as a cat dragging its new litter.

''So?'' Lana said.

''Lana, I got those two together so I can get a picture, and I want you in it. Three legends of the silver screen.''

''Oh, please!''

"Lana, isn't that why you gave me your camera, dear?"

"Oh, shit!" Resigned to the inevitable, she rose up regally, strode over to where Ginger and Lucille were waiting, and literally did a Loretta Young sweep into their presence. "Hi, girls! How're you doing?"

After the briefest exchange of pleasantries, I quickly got the shot before any of them changed their minds. Coup! Coup! Coup!

Later I discovered the value of my picture. Lucille and Ginger had not been photographed together since their days on the old RKO lot, where they were rivals and Lucille, via Desilu, eventually became the studio's owner.

Considering their past history, in the picture Lucille and Ginger actually look like friends. What great acting. Lana, however, appears to be in another world, forever the ice goddess, looking directly into the camera as though alone.

*A*fter Lana's horrible experience on the escalator, we were invited to yet another star party. Lana didn't want to go and insisted I take her back to our suite at The Plaza so she could rest.

"You go on back and have a good time, honey." She knew how I looked forward to cocktails and dancing—especially dancing.

When I returned to our designated table, Anne Baxter was waiting. "Where's Lana?" she asked.

"She isn't coming back. She's at the hotel resting because she's tired."

"Oh, yes. That's been her line for many years."

"Miss Baxter—"

"Call me Anne."

"—I'm here to have a good time and the only thing I'm missing at this time is a good dance partner."

"Bullshit. I'm a great dancer." She was a little high, so we took to the dance floor doing the Salsa and several other hot dances. She was, indeed, a great dancer.

Feeling guilty about Lana, alone at the hotel, I knew I'd have to cut my evening short. Before departing, however, Anne Baxter paid me a lovely compliment. "Why don't you start escorting me around instead of Lana?" She slipped her phone number into my pocket and bid me good-night.

Lana waited up for me. She'd been drinking and wanted to talk. The television droned on but she didn't seem interested. Nothing could have prepared me for what came next.

20

Good Friday

1958

"I killed the son-of-a-bitch and
I'd do it again!"

*W*e were sitting in our suite at The Plaza Hotel watching a television documentary on Hollywood scandals. Actually, we really weren't paying that much attention. Suddenly images of Lana, Johnny Stompanato, and Cheryl flashed across the screen.

"Lana, do you want me to shut it off?" I asked.

"No," she said. She watched intently until the narrator went on to somebody else's scandal, then clicked the remote. The screen went black.

She became extremely agitated and angry. Neither of us spoke for what seemed like a long time. Finally she blurted it out. "I killed the son-of-a-bitch and I'd do it again!"

"What!" I exclaimed, shocked.

"Scratch that," she said, making a waving gesture.

I wasn't sure I caught the enormity of what she said, but I immediately got the connection. Johnny Stompanato and the sensational murder at 730 North Bedford Drive on Good Friday in 1958. I thought the subject to be closed.

A couple of hours later she said, "How I'm suffering because of this."

"Because of what?" I asked.

"Cheryl. I owe her so much. I've done so many things wrong in my life I've had to live with but, darling, if I die before my daughter, you should tell the truth so I can rest in peace. Don't let my baby take the rap all her life for my mistake. I'll tell you something else, Eric. I do trust you. I'm sorry I blanked out earlier about the Stompanato thing on television. You know, I was so angry when Harold Robbins wrote *Where Love Has Gone*."

"Why? It was only a novel."

"Because I didn't want to face the truth. I blocked it out of my mind. You know I do that whenever I don't want to think about something that troubles me. The wall goes up and that's it. Nothing gets through. You've seen it all too many times. But now you know. I've spoken to you and said things I've never told anyone else, until tonight."

I saw and felt Lana's pain. I stopped her. "Lana, I don't want you to say another word. Stop it. It hurts me too much to see you in pain."

"All right," she said, "we won't talk about it. But remember, you're the only one who can set the record straight. Tell it. Someday, when I'm gone—tell it all."

It was three in the morning. I didn't sleep until almost daybreak, my mind and heart heavy for Lana, for her sense of guilt.

In the months and years ahead, Lana would let slip fragments of that awful night, and I began to put the pieces together. For instance, she told me that Cheryl did not go down to the kitchen and take a knife out of the drawer before "supposedly" murdering Johnny. "I kept that knife in the nightstand. The one by my bed."

Testimony at the inquest indicated that Johnny's body fell just inside Lana's bedroom, by the door where the police found him. Yet Lana's conversations with me on several occasions revealed that he was actually stabbed in her bed. None of this made any sense, because some of the parts were missing. She mentioned the verbal threats and physical abuse at the hands of Johnny Stompanato. She had even caught him in bed with another woman.

I had read about Cheryl and her rebellious activities immediately following the Stompanato killing: her temporary incarceration in Juvenile Hall, running away from the El Retiro Reform School, and the eventual awarding of her custody to her grandmother, Mildred.

If Lana had told me the truth, then it became

much easier to understand Cheryl's incredible behavior, post-Stompanato.

Johnny Stompanato was one of small-time
gangster Mickey Cohen's gunsels. Mickey's celebrity
had more to do with his connections to movie stars
than to Chicago mobsters. Mickey, however, knew
how to milk the publicity cow, and created his own
celebrity.

Stompanato had a reputation for bilking and
beating women. He was a punk—not a big-time
gangster. He preyed on weak, lonesome, desperate,
wealthy women, and some wealthy men. He used
the alias "Johnny Steele" in his "business" dealings.

Under the respectable cover of a gift shop in
Westwood, he had his fingers into a lot of pots,
mostly illegal in nature. A known pimp and hustler,
some insiders fingered him as the "hit man" when
John "the Enforcer" Whalen went down one evening in a San Fernando Valley Restaurant in the
1950s.

The police knew Stompanato and kept an eye on
him. As a matter of fact, Freddie Otash, the famous
Hollywood private eye, once a member of the
L.A.P.D. gangster squad before he left the department and hung out a shingle, often reported Johnny's mischief to Mickey Cohen, who, in turn, gave
Freddie information on his rivals in criminal circles.

Stompanato had been twice married and divorced; once to actress Helene Stanley, whose face
and figure were copied by artists at the Walt Disney

Studios to create Cinderella and Sleeping Beauty. Although the names of many celebrity women were found in Stompanato's little black book, Lana emerged as his most important prey. Lana, an astute judge of her public image, deplored bad press. Even as she found herself entangled in this mobster's web, she knew enough never to be seen with him at any career function.

During the weeks preceding his death, they had many arguments, some physically abusive, because she repeatedly refused to allow him to escort her to the Academy Awards, having been nominated for Best Actress in *Peyton Place*.

Stompanato, forced to relinquish what he considered to be his right, seethed. Lana's mother and daughter accompanied her to the Oscars and they sat at a table with Sean Connery, Johnny's long-time nemesis.

Many years would go by before I received corroboration of Lana's confession, from two separate and involved sources in particular. First, and probably the most important, came indirectly from Freddie Otash through Ray Strait, his biographer and friend for twenty-five years. A graphic inside story emerges from his notes and conversations with Otash, which are included in a forthcoming book, *Fred Otash—The Whole Truth!*, excerpted below:

Lana Turner's attorney, Jerry Geisler, summoned Fred to her swank Beverly Hills home in the middle of the night on Good Friday, 1958.

GEISLER: Get the hell over here. We've got a bloody mess on our hands.

OTASH: What're you talking about? What happened?

GEISLER: Stompanato's dead. There's blood all over the place—the bed looks like somebody butchered a hog in it.

When Fred arrived at Lana's Bedford Drive home, Lana was hysterical. He was not surprised that a tragedy had taken place. For months he had been working for Stephen Crane, one of Lana's former husbands and the father of her daughter, Cheryl. Crane hired him to find out how deeply involved his daughter was with Lana's two-bit gangster boyfriend. . . .

Fred stabled some horses in the San Fernando Valley where Stompanato had been teaching Cheryl to ride. . . . According to Fred, the only ride that interested Johnny was fucking Cheryl. On several occasions he'd observed them together from a distance . . . and to quote Fred directly, "He was all over her like skin." When he reported his findings back to Crane he was furious and a meeting was called between him, Otash and Lana . . .

The meeting took place at Crane's Luau Restaurant in Beverly Hills . . .

When Fred confronted Lana with hard evidence she refused to believe it . . . and stomped out in a rage . . .

At Lana's home, Geisler had already begun to orchestrate the crime scene when Fred arrived, and for a full two hours before the police were called, the two men got busy and did what they had to do to protect Lana . . .

Fred confirmed the blood and gore. . . . Although Johnny's body was discovered near the door, Fred said that he died in Lana's bed. "Jerry told me that Lana had walked in on Cheryl and Johnny . . . and that Lana went berserk and before either of them could get off the bed, she came down over them with a butcher knife. The kid was lucky. Johnny took the hit."

". . . I changed the prints myself. . . ." Fred said.

Lana was running around screeching, "My career! What's going to happen to my career?" . . .

Someone tipped Clinton Anderson, the Beverly Hills Chief of Police, that Fred had taken the knife out of Stompanato, cleaned Lana's prints off, and replaced them with Cheryl's. . . . He brought Fred into his office and threatened to charge him as an accessory to cover up a homicide. Fred claimed to have some damaging political information on Clinton and told me, "That's the only reason he never booked me. I know he got his information from someone in Lana's household because Geisler could have lost his license and so could I—and we'd both be doing a long stretch up the road if it could be proved. Neither of us talked."

When Geisler was in the hospital just prior to his

death, he asked to see Fred. In his hospital room he told Fred, "Don't ever talk about this as long as I'm alive."

"Nor as long as I'm alive," Fred laughed.

$\mathscr{K}$aren Kondazian, an award-winning actress who has had a notable career performing Tennessee Williams's plays as well as those of other playwrights, became a good friend of mine some fifteen years ago. It wasn't until 1995 that Karen informed me she and Lex Barker had been seriously involved at the time of his death in 1973. Karen had some quite specific feelings about Lex and what he related to her about Lana and Stompanato and that whole mess.

First of all, Cheryl claimed in her book, *Detour*, that Lex Barker repeatedly abused her sexually long before she finished junior high school. Knowing Lex as she did, Karen said that could never have been the case. She said that Lex, ever the perfect gentleman (and nearly thirty years older than Karen), was terribly self-conscious about the opinions of others regarding the age difference between them. "He was kind and gentle in every aspect of our relationship. Never did he force or insinuate himself in any improper way. He treated me with respect. He had grown children older than I, and even at his mature age, still so attractive, Lex never had to force himself on anyone. He did say Cheryl was always a problem, so jealous of her mother and desirous of gaining her mother's attention that she would flaunt her body before him. Lex repeatedly told Lana that Cheryl was going to cause her a lot of trouble someday.''

Cheryl's account states that she finally confronted her mother, at age thirteen, with her allegations against Lex, at which point Lana reputedly showed Lex the door. Their divorce followed soon after. Nonetheless, Lana and Lex remained friends.

Years later Lana told me, ''When Cheryl made her allegations against Lex, I had no choice but to believe her. I couldn't take the chance. Had it been true, and found out, my career would have been finished for allowing him to stay under the same roof. But more importantly, Cheryl deserved my protection. Truthfully, I always had doubts about Cheryl's accusations.''

Karen Kondazian revealed to me that Lex spoke to Lana in the days immediately following Stompanato's murder. Lana admitted to him that in the panic and hysteria of saving her career, she allowed Cheryl to take the blame for own misdeed. But she indicated strongly to Lex that Cheryl was not without blame. This confirmed Lex's earlier warnings that Cheryl would bring serious trouble to her mother.

✦ 21 ✦

Detour

1 9 8 8

"**How** dare she!"

Lana spat the words across the living room of her condo.

"Who the fuck does she think she is? How could she do this to me? My own daughter!"

She was referring, of course, to Cheryl's autobiography, *Detour*, whose publication she had dreaded since Cheryl first dropped the bombshell in her lap. "Mother, I'm writing my version of my life," Cheryl had said.

For months Lana had hoped the blow would not be too severe. She never prepared for the devastating impact her daughter's printed words would have on her. Although Cheryl may have tried to be fair and objective in her perspective, what emerged depicted Lana in the most unflattering portrait of a movie star since Christina Crawford raked her mother, Joan, across the coals in her book *Mommie Dearest*.

Cheryl never accused her mother of physical abuse or any of the other obvious comparisons to Miss Crawford; she only pictured her as the most vain, selfish, self-absorbed mother since Marlene Dietrich.

The publication of *Detour* devastated Lana so severely that she literally took to her bed for six months, the onset period of six years in seclusion.

Lana felt if you dignified something you hated with a response, you attracted public attention. When Cheryl started hitting the talk show circuit and sales of the book skyrocketed, Lana pretended the book didn't exist. Throughout the firestorm surrounding Cheryl's revelations, Lana made only one public statement. In a carefully worded press release, she said, "I think it took guts to write it."

She never, ever remarked about it in public again. Every interviewer beseeched Cheryl for direct comments from her mother. Cheryl, according to Lana, proceeded to invent these comments out of whole cloth, pretending they enjoyed a close mother-daughter relationship.

On one particular occasion I watched, totally fascinated, as Lana Turner's daughter fielded some tough personal questions from Jane Wyman's daughter, Maureen Reagan. The "Falcon Crest" debacle never surfaced, but Maureen viewed the book with a degree of skepticism.

Cheryl, a few years earlier, had refused permission to allow a depiction of herself in a television movie based on Lana's autobiography. Planning with great anticipation a movie version of her own book, producer Alan Carr optioned the rights to *Detour* and launched a personal campaign to woo Lana's endorsement and permission to use her name. He didn't realize how unmovable Lana could and would be in this particular instance.

"She refused me permission when I wanted to make my book into a movie," Lana declared. "I guarantee they'll never film her book as long as I'm alive."

Undaunted, Alan Carr had a huge spray of flowers in the form of a horseshoe delivered to Lana's Ivory Tower while she and I were watching television one day. She took one look at the card, glanced at the ostentatious floral display, snorted, and threw the greeting in the wastebasket.

Along with the flowers came an offer to be a guest presenter at the 1988 Academy Awards ceremony being produced by Carr. He assured Lana that she would be presented in legendary fashion, singled out as "one of a kind." She declined, which turned out to be one of her smarter moves, because that particular Oscar presentation, featuring Rob Lowe doing "snow" jokes with Disney's "Snow White," went down as the worst edition in Oscar history. It has become "the" Oscar joke of all times.

Cheryl's movie deal with Alan Carr eventually went into turnaround and the project languished. Talk of a miniseries also evaporated. Lana showed satisfaction when she told me that she'd been personally responsible for Cheryl not appearing on the cover of *People* magazine. They'd insisted on mother and daughter appearing together. Lana nixed it, which infuriated Cheryl.

One of the things in the book that disturbed Lana most was Cheryl's open admission of her lesbian lifestyle with her lover, Josh. She didn't want to be confronted again with the old bugaboo of being a "bad mother."

It puzzled her that Cheryl would dig up the Lex Barker incident, too. She saw no reason for that. People had forgotten him. "It's just another way of getting back at me. Why," she asked, "is she doing this to me?"

Despite Lana's refusal to participate, Alan Carr and Cheryl resurrected their plans to make the movie. Cheryl went on record as saying she thought Madonna would be an excellent choice to play Lana who, upon hearing this, shrieked in my presence, "Over my dead body!"

Lana loathed Madonna's sexual theatrics. We were watching one of Madonna's music videos on MTV when Lana said, "She does have some talent and musical ability, but why does she have to cheapen herself with all the sex and lust and porno mentality?"

The furor over *Detour* ended any warmth or respect that might have been rekindled between Lana and Cheryl. She never forgave being branded in print by her own daughter as the vain and selfish woman she was, in fact, capable of being. Lana continued to have me join her when she occasionally had dinner with Cheryl and Josh. Although she never forgave Cheryl, she still saw her daughter from time to time.

In late 1990 Cheryl prepared a beautiful dinner for us at the home she shared with Josh on Doheny Drive, above Sunset, once the heart of youthful Hollywood. Excited, she told her mother that she had been asked to write a real estate column for the *Los Angeles Times*.

"What is this?" Lana asked. "Why would you want to do that? Do you have to have a column in order to drop the names of your celebrity clients?"

"Mother, I'm doing it because I'm in real estate and it would be good for business."

"Oh, Cheryl, grow up. Why demean yourself? You're above this."

Lana went out to the back patio and started puffing on a cigarette. I felt sorry for Cheryl. She stood with tears in her eyes by the stove, stirring a skillet of gravy.

"She's always been this way. She never gives me her love and support," Cheryl told me.

"I don't understand your mother's behavior," I said, putting my arms around her. "I think it's wonderful that you have a chance to do this column."

She fled to the bathroom in tears.

I went out to the patio and said, "Lana, why don't you go inside and embrace your daughter?

Make peace. She's proud of the opportunity and wanted to share her happiness with you."

Lana wouldn't budge.

"Maybe if she gets rid of that super ego we could have a decent conversation."

I thought to myself, *she certainly had a good role model*. Lana showed herself to be the total bitch that evening.

"Cheryl," I said later, "I know your mother loves you."

"Eric, I'd rather not talk about it."

At the dinner table, arguments aside, Lana displayed a healthy appetite. Cheryl, however, didn't eat at all. Josh and I were at a loss for words and the subject of Cheryl's newspaper column never surfaced again in my presence.

The last time I took Lana to Cheryl and Josh's house for dinner, Lily Tomlin and Jane Wagner were the only other invited guests. It was Thanksgiving 1991. I tried not to show the hurt I felt when Lana told me later that Cheryl had said, "Mother, do you have to bring Eric? We just don't think he'll fit in with this evening."

Lana said she had been as direct as possible with Cheryl, saying, "Darling, if you don't want Eric, you don't want me, and I would just as soon not come at all."

Remembering those words gives me a special feeling of pride—that she stood up for me to her own daughter. I felt like family. I truly was her brother that night. We had a great time.

The last argument I recall between Cheryl and Lana occurred during yet another evening when Cheryl begged her mother, who no longer signed autographs, to please endorse a photograph for Madonna. Lana said, "No. I don't sign autographs."

"Mother, please. She asked me if you would do this." She'd recently met Madonna at a party. Madonna owned a rare photo of Lana in a funky 1940s get-up, so stunning it almost seemed contemporary.

"Please, mother. Please."

Lana finally gave in. "Oh, all right, give it to me."

She signed the picture, to the best of my recollection, "From one gutsy broad to another."

For the next several weeks she showed her disgust for having broken her rule by signing the picture.

"Why," she asked me, "did you let me do it? You know how I feel about Madonna. Why did I do it?"

Nor were matters improved when, a few days later, Lana received a personally inscribed photo from Madonna. She looked at me and rolled her eyes and said, "Did I ask for this?"

In any event, Lana had been correct when she'd referred to Madonna as "one gutsy broad."

22

Miss Turner Regrets

*W*ith her career sliding, her comeback now history, Lana became more and more reclusive. I continued to show up at her apartment to take care of her hair, as did my sister to do her nails. Lana was rapidly becoming the Norma Desmond of Century Park East.

It became increasingly difficult for my sister and me to adjust to Lana's self-imposed exile. She still received, and did up until her death, invitations to all of Hollywood's important functions. She passed them on to me, simply penning her regrets to the host or hostess, or had me convey them in person.

She almost didn't show for a tribute given her by the Thalians, founded by Lana's old friend Debbie Reynolds, who continues to be its biggest booster. It took all the skill my friend Gloria Luckenbill and I possessed to coerce Lana into appearing, which she eventually did—but not until very late in the evening.

On other occasions, those waiting to see Lana in the flesh were not so fortunate. She skipped a big evening, planned far in advance, at one of Beverly Hills' most popular nightclubs, La Cage aux Folles, where we were supposed to share a table with Sammy and Altovise Davis and their party. As the night wore on, people stopped expecting to see her. I arrived without Lana, with what by now had become my standard apology. Sammy reached over, patted my arm, and said, "I know. You don't even have to tell me. She's not going to make it. She's famous for this. She's always done it. It's getting worse. Don't worry about it, Eric. Kick back and have a good time with us."

I felt equally guilty when Lana failed to appear as the guest of honor at a charity benefit for handicapped children, arranged by my good friend, actress/dancer Zena Bethune. Words cannot express the anger and frustration I felt at Lana's cruelty. People bought tickets just to see Lana Turner.

My biggest disappointment came the night I missed an opportunity to spend an evening at Barbra Streisand's house. Through my friendship with Barbra's mother and sister Rosalyn Kind, Lana received an invitation to a fabulous party Barbra was giving at her mansion on Carolwood Drive in Holmby Hills. I became ecstatic. Any invitation to Lana automatically included me. Everyone knew that.

After taking her sweet time to decide, Lana finally said, "Yeah, we'll go." She didn't show much enthusiasm, which caused me concern. I knew Lana liked—no, loved—Barbra's singing. Her favorite song was "People."

"But, Lana," I said, "you're a loner, so why would you love a song about people?"

"That's bullshit. I'm not a loner and you know it!"

"Well, whatever. Let's go to the party and have a great time, okay? You can tell Barbra personally how much you like the song."

As the night of the party grew near, Lana ceased talking about it. I started to get nervous, afraid she was going to back out once again at the last minute. I called to remind her several days ahead of time and she told me not to worry, that we'd go and have a great time. Early on the evening of the party I called her from my home.

"I'm getting dressed, Lana. I'll be at your apartment in twenty minutes to pick you up."

"Okay," she said flatly.

When I arrived she began to put on her makeup very, very slowly, and spoke in a monotone. I would not allow Lana to dampen my enthusiasm by her lack of it. To cap it all off, Lana's arrival had been planned as a big surprise for Barbra, who, according to her sister, also greatly admired Lana.

I sat in a chair near the foyer of Lana's apartment, waiting, and waiting, and still waiting.

"Lana," I finally said, looking at my watch, "we're already forty-five minutes late."

"Eric! You know how I hate being rushed! In fact"—uh-oh, here it comes—"I'm not even in the mood to go."

"But Lana —"

"That's why we're such close friends, my darling. Because you know me and understand me. You know what's in my heart." She had cold feet. She knew she didn't look her best, and Lana never wanted to be "second best."

"Lana, I've been looking forward to this. You know that."

She shrugged. "Go without me." She attempted to appear sympathetic, but I wasn't having any of that. Truth is, I did know her and I knew when she was acting, and believe me, this was an act.

Okay, lady, back in your face, I decided. "No, Lana, you're more important to me than any Barbra Streisand party. I'll stay here and watch television with you."

Sure I was pissed, but loyalty ruled my heart. I stayed home and we watched the story of our lives—a big prime-time soap opera.

There we were—I, dressed to the teeth in formal wear, and she, in her "lady about the house" coat. We sat up side by side on her bed, like two fossils, watching the tube.

When she finally got the courage to turn and look at me, I realized she had one eyebrow on and one off. She hadn't gotten very far with her makeup.

"Darling," I cooed, "did you know you forgot one of your eyebrows?"

"Well," she said petulantly, "since I'm sitting to your left and my right eyebrow is on, I just won't turn my head to talk to you. I'll just look straight ahead and then you won't have to suffer my missing eyebrow."

As the evening wore on, she knew I was miserable and would rather be at Barbra Streisand's party. "God, you're fidgety," she said, *fidgety* being one of her favorite words.

After what seemed like hours of pretending to be comfortable, Lana made an announcement. "Eric, you are not good company tonight. My darling brother, I am tired. I want to go to bed. But you can still go to Barbra's party."

She knew quite well that I couldn't. It was a dinner party and dinner was now over.

"Oh, Lana, I would never do that without you." I practically choked on the words.

"Oh, what an understanding brother you are. That's why I love you so. You always do the right thing."

She tried to brainwash me—again—with her "act." I wasn't into it. "Well, darling, I'll go on home now," I said, not bothering to hide my feelings.

"Oh, sweetheart. Don't act so disappointed." She

pushed now, rubbing it in my face with all the drama she could muster.

"No, dear, I'm really not disappointed. We'll have other exciting nights together. I love you."

With some effort I kissed her on both cheeks. She gave me a hug so strong it told me she had a guilty conscience. *Good*, I thought. *Let her feel bad.* I certainly did.

As I left her apartment, Lana stood in the doorway, looking as concerned as humanly possible with only one eyebrow, like some bizarre incarnation of Cruella DeVille. The impression lasted—and my sides didn't burst into laughter until I was on the elevator down to the first floor. Lana had a grotesque sense of humor, and I still don't know if she knew that.

*A*lthough my sister, Harriet, did Lana's nails for almost ten years, she found it increasingly difficult to put up with Lana's crude behavior when she drank. More and more, drinking seemed to fill the emptiness in Lana's life.

Harriet desperately tried to get to Lana's apartment before the drinking began. She genuinely liked a sober Lana, who could be kind, loving, and thoughtful. A drunk Lana, on the other hand, could be difficult, opinionated, and nasty. Lana knew Harriet—a born-again Christian—had been trying to get me closer to the Lord. Salting the wound, Lana would sometimes deliberately bait Harriet with her metaphysical beliefs. I found her behavior offensive.

One time Harriet arrived to find Lana and her secretary glued to Lana's big-screen television, watching Shirley MacLaine. The two women greeted Shirley's every word with "oohs" and "ahhhs."

After a few moments Lana turned to Harriet and said, "You really don't believe in this, do you?"

"No."

"I can tell, because you're not saying anything."

"It's against God," Harriet finally said. "Man is appointed once to die, then the judgment. He's not supposed to come back and come back and come back. It's in the Bible."

"Well, I don't believe in the Bible," Lana said, deliberately trying to arouse Harriet's ire. "Shirley MacLaine *is* a god!"

"Oh? And who appointed Shirley MacLaine a god?" my sister asked.

"We're all gods," Lana said.

"There's only one God. God the Father, the Son, and the Holy Spirit."

"The Bible was written by man," Lorry Sherwood, Lana's secretary, chimed in.

Harriet, ready for her, said, "Shirley MacLaine's book was written by Shirley MacLaine."

Lana, unable to make a response for the moment, used the expression she always used when she failed to win her point. "Please, let's not get into this."

A few months later, the movie *Postcards From the*

Edge came out, based on the book by Debbie Reynolds's daughter, Carrie Fisher. In the film, Shirley MacLaine's character makes a very derogatory and insulting remark about Lana Turner.

I took Lana to see the film. It infuriated her. "But, Lana," I said, "it's only a movie. It's dialogue she's supposed to say. It's not real."

"I don't care. She made me look like a tramp. She didn't have to say that. If Debbie were truly my friend, she would never have said that about me."

The next time Harriet visited Lana, knowing of the *Postcards* incident, she asked, "Well, what do you think of your God now?" Later Harriet brought Lana a copy of a Christian parody of one of Shirley's books called *Out on a Broken Limb.*

$\mathcal{M}$y sister was quite startled to hear Lana's views on reincarnation after Lana and I returned from our Egypt trip. Lana insisted she was the reincarnation of none other than the Queen of Egypt, Cleopatra herself.

"Isn't it amazing," Harriet said to Lana, "that there are so many Cleopatras walking around today? No one ever comes back after being a slave or handmaiden. By the way, Lana, how do you know you were once Cleopatra?"

Lana stared directly into her eyes and calmly said, "Because I am Lana Turner."

Harriet looked across Lana's crystal coffee table,

laden with pyramids, unicorns, flying saucers, and other symbols of a mystical nature. She understood Lana's bad health and, looking at these symbols, she asked, "Are these working for you, Lana?"

Lana never looked up. "Not yet."

"And they never will. These are crystal and glass objects. You're worshiping the creation, Lana, not the Creator."

Lana forgave Harriet their differences of opinion regarding religion because Harriet gave her nails the most beautiful manicure she had ever received. Her vanity allowed room for God. Whether or not she'd admit it, Lana had more faith than she wanted anyone to know about. At least I hope she did.

Lana's fingernails curled under like claws and had been a problem all her life. Using a special silicon formula, Harriet changed their contour, causing them to curve naturally. The *National Enquirer* subsequently did a story on Lana's fingernails, exaggerating by saying she paid $100 a session and had them done every single week. Both statements were untrue.

"I wish you did have me do them every week and I do wish you paid me one hundred dollars," Harriet said.

Lana expressed her most sincere feelings when she thanked Harriet. "This is the only time in my career anyone ever did an article about my nails being so beautiful."

$\mathcal{N}$ot only did Lana begin refusing all invitations to public and private events, but there were also long periods of time when she wouldn't leave her condo. Groceries, drugs, and liquor would be delivered, and Carmen and I would bring her anything else she might need.

During the last two years I was with her, we went out only a total of four or five times, including the memorable Thanksgiving spent with Cheryl, Josh, Lily Tomlin, and Jane Wagner. Lana now preferred quiet dinners under controlled circumstances where she wouldn't have to worry about her makeup or being photographed. Her only public outing during this period was when I took her to a performance of *Oba Oba*, the dynamic Brazilian musical review. Lana loved the show and, in a rare departure from her recent behavior, she even went backstage to pose for pictures with the cast. It was one of the last times she would do so.

I began to think it was going to take an act of God or some natural catastrophe to get her out of the Ivory Tower more often. As it turned out, my prediction was not far off.

Shortly after 1 A.M. on a Tuesday morning, I awoke with a shock. I was in bed in Lana's guest room when flashes of light and distorted bursts of noise interrupted my sleep. Since we were at the very top of the high-rise, I knew something was seriously wrong. Hearing the sound of a siren from somewhere below, I pulled open the drapes and saw flames shooting up the side of the building beneath our floor. Several fire trucks were heading down Olympic Boulevard in our direction.

I ran into Lana's room. She was asleep, sitting up in bed with her head slumped forward. The television was still on.

"Lana, wake up!"

"What?" she said with a start. "What is it? What's wrong?"

"There's a fire in the building!"

"I don't believe you!"

"Well, then, look," I said, staring toward her window.

"Eric, don't open the drapes!" she shouted. In her paranoid fantasies she was always afraid someone from the north tower of the building was looking at her apartment through binoculars, trying to catch a glimpse of her without her makeup or every hair in place.

Disregarding her instructions, I threw back the curtains. "Look at that! Are you blind?"

She saw the unmistakable traces of flames and rotating lights from emergency vehicles. A helicopter buzzed overhead. "Oh my God! What are we going to do?"

"We're getting the hell out of here!" I yelled.

"No, I can't," she cried. "I'm not dressed or made up!"

"So what?"

Suddenly an announcement boomed from a public address system: "The elevators are not in use. Please proceed calmly to the nearest stairway and evacuate the building."

"But we're on the twentieth floor!" she shrieked. "I am not walking down all those flights. I'm not leaving!"

"I don't believe you," I said incredulously.

"It's probably a small fire, anyway."

"Lana, take another look outside. It's reaching your windows!" By now I was seriously frightened and afraid I wouldn't be able to get her to leave. "You can stay here if you want, but I'm getting out!"

"But my hair! My face! I didn't even have a chance to put on my eyebrows!"

"That's too damn bad," I said, determined not to become a human marshmallow for the sake of her vanity.

"Please exit your apartments immediately!" came the second announcement. "Proceed calmly to the nearest stairway."

"Get your ass over here! You're going with me," I demanded.

Finally scared into submission, she hastily organized a comical disguise in which she could leave the building "unnoticed." "Get my babushka, my scarf, and my fur wrap," she ordered, darting about the room. Somehow, we managed to get the babushka on, the fur wrap over the babushka, and the scarf over her hair. Before I pushed her out the door she also managed to grab her huge, oversized dark glasses. We were heading into the stairwell when she said, "I forgot to lock the door!"

"Forget the door and start thinking about our lives!"

"But, Eric," she whimpered.

"You have insurance, don't you?"

"Yes."

"Are your diamonds in there?"

"No."

"Then forget it. We're not going back." We continued down the stairs with Lana grasping the railing in one hand and my arm in the other.

As we passed the various landings, other evacuees joined us, including several elderly women in nightgowns and hair nets. One little lady was terribly shaken. Lana immediately put her arms around her. "Sweetheart, don't be scared. We'll be all right," she said, comforting the woman.

For the moment she had overcome her own fears and forgotten her appearance. I was briefly seeing a side of her that always amazed me: her surprising strength during a crisis.

Once we reached the lobby it was a different story. The building entrance was swarming with reporters and photographers from the *Los Angeles Times* and several local TV stations. Lana was terrified that she'd be recognized.

Suddenly an actress who also lived in the building

came running toward us. "Oh, Lana, are you all right?" she screeched. At the mere mention of Lana's name, several photographers turned away from the fire and started to come our way. Lana grabbed me and started pulling me outside toward a cluster of trees near the driveway.

"Eric, stand in front of me! Don't let them see me! If anyone asks, tell them I've been sick with the flu and that you had to get me out of bed."

I did as I was told, shielding her as much as possible. When a reporter actually did get close enough to speak to her, Lana berated him for focusing on her when there was a "much more serious issue at hand." She was still facing the trees, refusing to turn around for fear the man might snap her picture. Eventually he gave up and drifted away.

With the help of the building security office and a rescue unit, we were finally able to call a cab, which took us to the Marriott Hotel three blocks away. We checked in around 3 A.M. without so much as a toothbrush or a comb in our possession. Luckily the hotel saw to our needs, and we finally got to sleep as dawn was breaking across the southland.

When we returned to Lana's apartment for an inspection the following day, we discovered that her balcony had been scorched and there was a good deal of smoke damage. The condo association announced that her unit would be cleaned and painted as soon as possible.

On a sadder note, the apartment next to Lana's had been completely gutted by the fire. The elderly couple who lived there had perished in the flames.

As Lana grew more and more reclusive, telephones and television became her major conduits to the outside world. She watched TV incessantly. Her favorite programs were, not surprisingly, glossy melodramas and soap operas like "Dallas" and "Dynasty"—reminders of the kinds of films she used to make. She also enjoyed "Murder She Wrote," which often featured stars of her era, if not her caliber. She had nothing but the highest regard for Angela Lansbury, who had once costarred with her in *The Three Musketeers* at MGM.

During the last weeks I was with her, Lana spent much of her time watching the O.J. Simpson double murder trial unfold on the giant TV screen in her living room. Ever since the infamous low-speed Bronco chase she'd been engrossed in every detail. On more than one occasion news reports had referred to the crime as the most sensational celebrity murder case since the Lana Turner–Johnny Stompanato scandal. She smirked at these comparisons but remained glued to the continuing coverage.

Lana's take on the situation was quite different from that of the average viewer. After all, this was the world-renowned celebrity who, in 1958, had hired her own "dream team" to exonerate her from a killing that had shocked the world. Lana had been a bigger star then than O.J. Simpson was now, and attorney Jerry Geisler was easily the Johnnie Cochran of his day.

During one of our last phone conversations, shortly before the Simpson trial was set to begin, I asked Lana what she thought of his chances for acquittal.

"He's got the best defense money can buy," she said. "He'll get off."

And who should know better?

*A*s Lana withdrew from public life, her health began to fail again. Her consumption of alcohol increased. She kept three one-gallon jugs of Chardonnay in her refrigerator at all times. She had her first glass for breakfast when she arose around three in the afternoon, and the last before retiring as the sun crept over the horizon.

She no longer had a career, only she didn't know it. There would always be, she said, a cameo, a television show. She believed that. Reality spoke otherwise.

She still received huge royalty checks from her profit participation in *Imitation of Life*. I remember one particular day when she received two separate checks, for the video and foreign distribution, respectively.

At this juncture, despite her drinking, failing health, and inactivity, Lana decided to make a "career switch."

Laurino Scaffone, an artist friend of mine since my boyhood days in Detroit, had become an accomplished artist, painting beautiful historical landscapes on thin slabs of marble. When Lana saw photographs of his work she became philanthropic for the first time in her life. She gave him $23,000 to assist in the continuation of his work and prepare enough pieces for a show. She now considered herself a patron of the arts.

We prepared several portfolios featuring beautiful color photographs of his art, prefaced with letters of introduction from Lana herself. I personally presented these to all the major galleries in Los Angeles. Lana planned to host his exclusive Los Angeles showing at the Tamara Bane Gallery.

Several other Beverly Hills art galleries expressed similar interest. Lana decided to make use of her extensive show business connections by sending handwritten invitations to celebrity friends such as Frank Sinatra, Elizabeth Taylor, and others. She was calling in her markers. She'd never done that before. She even designed the dress she would wear to the opening. Sincerely excited, she spoke to the artist on the phone late at night after a day of drinking. She told him that she believed, although she had never met him in *this* life, that the two of them had once been lovers in another lifetime, inhabiting the landscapes he now painted.

Unfortunately, before Lana could make final arrangements for his introduction into Los Angeles art circles, she was diagnosed with throat cancer. Her own plans permanently shelved, she continued to encourage him, although the funding gradually ceased. She blamed her daughter. "Cheryl will kill me if she finds out I am sending him any more money."

She kept three of his pieces in her home until the day she died.

❧ 23 ❧

All That Glitters

LOS ANGELES, DECEMBER 1995

*N*ovember and December 1995 were curious and difficult months. With all the early plans finally coming together to put almost twenty-five years of my life into book form, I ask myself, now, is that all there is? Writing a book is, in a way, not unlike having a baby. The idea, the conception, the waiting and labor, and finally, the birth.

I notice the name of Lana Turner has begun to resurface throughout the media with a new surge of interest. Surfing the TV channels with my television remote control, I see that Lana's old movies are being dusted off and shown with more frequency. Christie's recently held a highly publicized auction of her jewelry at the Peninsula Hotel in Beverly Hills. The Los Angeles County Museum of Art launched a retrospective of her work, screening many of her important films.

The auction of Lana's jewels, coming four

months after her death, brought in roughly $200,000. I understand from friends who attended both the auction and the film exhibit that Lana's daughter, Cheryl, who supplied much of the information for Christie's catalog, received all proceeds from the sale. By the time commissions and taxes were paid, Lana's fabulous collection netted a fraction of its real value.

I thought for a moment about some of the pieces: the ring with the letter "L" in diamonds that she wore on our trip to Deauville, France; the diamond-and-turquoise bracelet gifted to her by the president of Mexico; the cabochon ruby-and-diamond ring from Frank Sinatra . . . all had been coldly dispensed of under the auctioneer's gavel.

Rumors still swirl. One contact informed me that a screenplay entitled *The Killing of Johnny Stompanato* is in the works, and Cheryl is supposedly working with writer Jeffrey Lane on the project, which I find hard to believe. It strikes me as odd that she would want to rake that tragedy over the coals one more time, unless it is for the money. I've also been told that Lana's condo—her Ivory Tower—will be kept for an indefinite period exactly as she left it.

And then there's speculation about Lana's last will and testament—who benefits, and just as importantly, who doesn't—and why. That remains a mystery as of this writing.

From the auction news it seems that Cheryl came into most of her mother's physical property, but the recipient of the bulk of the estate has not been publicly identified—yet. Perhaps the war between mother and daughter continues even after Lana's passing. I haven't a clue about that, but I'll bet Lana is still somehow pushing buttons and pulling strings—controlling from the grave all that involves her. I am amused.

I am not amused, however, about an article in the November 1995 issue of *The Lesbian News*. The cover features a photograph of Josh and Cheryl against a midnight-blue backdrop with a shimmering, ghostly image of Lana's face looming over them! The headline, just as eerie, reads: MOMMY MOVIESTAR. Maybe Lana had it right when she said that Hollywood has become just another trash bin.

That is the same article in which Cheryl is quoted as saying that, just before her mother died, Lana confessed that she, too, was a lesbian! I hope Cheryl never made such a statement about her mother, that it is some sort of misquote, because it simply wasn't true. As anyone who ever knew her will attest, Lana Turner was an overtly *blatant* heterosexual.

During the last few weeks of working on this book I've learned more about those who engineered Lana away from me right before she died. Extremely reliable friends of both myself and Lana tell me that two individuals who I once counted among my friends betrayed me. One is an entertainer and is fairly well-known on the Hollywood nightclub circuit. The other can be described only as a "Lanatic."

I wish I could say that these revelations came as a surprise to me. They didn't. Anger is the only emotion I feel.

The "Lanatic" and his mother used me to score points with Lana. They walked into my Beverly Hills salon several years ago and asked if I'd do their hair. The son told me he'd read of my close association with their favorite star, and that his mother wanted me to do her hair in Lana's color. I gave her something close to it and began what I thought would be another client friendship. Nothing more, nothing less.

With or without an appointment, the son kept dropping by and calling me, always asking about Lana and professing his great interest in her career. I thought of him as just a benign fan who enjoyed having a vicarious relationship with her. On one or two occasions he'd been in the salon when I'd spoken to Lana on the phone. He knew we spoke frequently.

Sometime in 1987 I became ill. After I had spent the better part of a year relocating and reopening my Beverly Hills salon, my energies were depleted, my spirits low. I was listless, run down, and aside from the fact that I knew I was drinking too much, I couldn't imagine why I was feeling this way. After an extensive series of blood tests it was determined that I was suffering from a bronchial infection. The prognosis was good. With strict nutritional guidance and herbal therapy I would be fine.

I deliberately avoided telling Lana about any of

this because I didn't want to alarm her, but she obviously could see that I wasn't well. When I failed to keep several of our regularly scheduled appointments, she started to worry.

Just as I had always supported her through her various illnesses with my advice and concern, she was determined to respond in kind. But first she had to find out what was wrong with me. She began by calling my friends to see if they knew.

A friend remembers coming home late one night and finding a series of urgent messages from Lana on his answering machine. Between her messages to him, Lana finally reached me at home, and I filled her in on my illness and proposed treatment. She was both concerned and relieved. After I assured her that everything would be all right, she left yet another message for him, explaining that I was home resting and he was not to disturb me.

Since he and I hadn't talked for several days and he had no idea I was even sick, he called Lana to get more information. Although it was after 1 A.M., she spent the next hour telling him how upset she'd been until she finally reached me. She'd been worried for days and if she hadn't finally gotten me on the phone that night, she was going to send him over to my apartment and have him break in, if necessary, to see if I was all right.

This was the concerned and loving side of my little sister—the thoughtful, motherly aspect of her personality that never failed to win me over, time and time again.

Eventually I moved to San Jacinto and opened a new salon in nearby Hemet, but I still spent half my time in Los Angeles with Lana.

One day the son phoned and invited me to a dinner party at his mountaintop home near Escondido. Standing on his terrace and marveling at the view, I heard the theme song from *Madame X* ("The Swedish Rhapsody") playing softly in the background. It just didn't occur to me at the time that I might be the victim of a set-up. The music only reminded me of how much I missed her and that we hadn't spoken in several days.

"Why don't you call her?" the son suggested eagerly. "You can use the phone inside."

A few minutes later I telephoned Lana, never thinking that by calling her long distance from his house, her number would appear on his next phone bill. Now he had Lana's private, unlisted phone number. A few weeks later *he* called her.

"Why would you give him my number?" she asked indignantly.

"Lana, I never give your phone number to anyone. I called you from his house. He obviously got your number from his phone bill. Have I ever given your phone number out to anyone without your permission?"

"Well, I should hope not."

From her brief remarks, I gathered that the guy

had actually kept her on the line for ten or fifteen minutes. He soon sent a note of apology and several gifts, and her attitude softened. Soon she gave him permission to call.

One day not long before Lana died, after I hadn't seen or spoken with her for several months, I spoke to Josh on the phone. She immediately asked me about Lana's "new fan." I sensed that, for some reason, she and Cheryl were concerned.

"Who is this guy?" she asked.

I told her what I knew, how he and his mother had befriended me to get close to Lana, and how he'd appropriated her phone number. I asked Josh, "Why do you want to know? Is there something wrong?"

"Because he's trying to take your place with Mom and remove you from the picture," she said. I began to get the uncomfortable feeling that we were discussing the plot of *All About Eve*.

"Josh, why won't she talk to me?" I asked the question straight and direct.

"We don't know, but we're trying to find out what's going on, and we *really* want to get you two back together. We miss you, Eric. You're family."

A short time later it became apparent that Lana's new "friends"—the nightclub performer and the "Lanatic"—were spreading malicious lies about me to Lana, accusing me of saying cruel things about Lana behind her back. That she could possibly have believed anything like that goes beyond all the warmth and trust we had between us for so many years. My hurt became almost unbearable.

In my last attempt to reach her, I sent Lana a soul-searching letter, beseeching her not to listen to troublemakers who would come between us. I reminded her of our deep, spiritual bond and, again, begged her to ignore gossip and lies. My last words were that I would always love her and would be praying for her constantly. She never saw the letter.

Today, my understanding is quite clear as to how Lana's surrogate "family" banded together, closed ranks, and locked me out of her life. Worst of all, Lana allowed it to happen.

And yet, she had become so ill and vulnerable, I wonder if she really had a choice. At times I've even told myself that she did it deliberately, knowing how emotional I can be, and didn't want me to endure the pain of watching her die. But that's only one of many thoughts I've had to consider.

My consolation comes from knowing that she spoke of me frequently and with affection during the months before she passed away. On the day she died she told Carmen, "I miss my brother and wish he were here."

*D*espite forty years of major stardom, the murder of Johnny Stompanato became the defining moment in Lana Turner's life. If what she told me—and if what others have verified—is true the world will never understand the price Cheryl Crane paid for her mother's career.

To most parents it would be unthinkable that a mother, under any circumstances, could allow her child to take the blame for a brutal murder she herself committed. Most parents are not Hollywood legends. There are no easy answers.

It's impossible to fully comprehend the fury that drove Lana on Good Friday, 1958, or to know how much Cheryl's behavior in the moments prior to the murder actually contributed to it. I've always gotten the impression from Lana that she blamed Cheryl as much as she did herself for what happened. It was implicit, not so much in what she said, but in the attitude she had toward her daughter for the rest of her life.

The last remaining link to the truth behind this sordid affair lies buried within the private memories of Cheryl Crane. For thirty-seven years she has not changed her version of the story in any substantial manner, but she may have come close. In *Detour* she recounts an incident wherein she tried to explain the murder to her lover, Josh. Although she later glosses over the conversation as though it were merely an attempt at wishful thinking, the words ring true.

"You know," she writes in the book, "I didn't do it. I love you so much more than anyone else in my life, Josh, that I don't want you to think I could do a terrible thing like that."

Did that one line confirm all that Lana told me?

That Fred Otash told his biographer? That Lex Barker told his lover?

*A*s for me, I've come to terms with what happened in 1995 and the past twenty-four years before that. I've forgiven any real or imagined grievances and, once again, I'm focusing on my own career, my family, and my loved ones.

When I think of Lana, for so many years my beloved "Little Sister," my heart is heavy, my thoughts in conflict. The sickly, selfish, manipulative woman she finally became seems merely an alcoholic impostor who bore little resemblance to the woman I first met. I remember my beautiful, loving, funny, *sober* friend and our many great adventures together.

I can't be totally objective, of course. Without knowing all the details behind Lana's greatest tragedy, I would never presume to condemn her. The Bible says, "Judge not, lest ye be judged," and I strongly believe in that time-tested wisdom. I don't think any of us has the right to pronounce a final verdict on the life of this amazing woman.

Leave her to heaven.

Bibliography

Cini, Zelda, and Bob Crane. *Hollywood: Land and Legend.* Westport, Conn.: Arlington House, 1980.

Crane, Cheryl, with Cliff Jahr. *Detour: A Hollywood Story.* New York: Arbor House/William Morrow, 1988.

Crowther, Bosley. *The Lion's Share.* New York: E. P. Dutton and Co., 1957.

Eames, John Douglas. *The MGM Story.* New York: Crown Publishers, 1979.

Fitzgerald, Michael. *Universal Pictures.* New Rochelle, N.Y.: Arlington House, 1977.

Gardner, Ava. *Ava: My Story.* New York: Bantam Books, 1990.

Heimann, Jim. *Out With the Stars.* New York: Abbeville Press, 1985.

Hirschhorn, Clive. *The Universal Story.* New York: Crown Publishers, 1983.

———. *The Warner Bros. Story.* New York: Crown Publishers, 1979.

Lawton, Richard. *A World of Movies.* New York: Dell Publishing Co., 1974.

Levin, Martin. *Hollywood and the Great Fan Magazines.* New York: Arbor House, 1970.

Michael, Paul. *The American Movies Reference Book: The Sound Era.* New Jersey: Prentice Hall, 1976.

Morella, Joe, and Edward Epstein. *Lana: The Public and Private Lives of Miss Turner.* New York: Dell Publishing Co., 1971.

Parrish, James Robert. *The Best of MGM*. Westport, Conn.: Arlington House, 1981.

Pero, Taylor, and Jeff Rovin. *Always Lana*. New York: Bantam Books, 1982.

Sennet, Ted. *Warner Brothers Presents*. New York: Castle Books, 1971.

Shiach, Don. *The Movie Book*. New York: Smithmark, 1995.

Shipman, David. *The Great Movie Stars*. New York: Bonanza Books, 1970.

Stallings, Penny. *Flesh and Fantasy*. New York: St. Martin's Press, 1978.

Trent, Paul, and Richard Lawton. *The Image Makers*. New York: McGraw-Hill, 1972.

Turner, Lana. *Lana: The Lady, the Legend, the Truth*. New York: E. P. Dutton and Co., 1982.

Valentino, Lou. *The Films of Lana Turner*. New York: Citadel Press, 1976.

Wayne, Jane Ellen. *Lana's Men: The Life and Loves of Lana Turner*. New York: St. Martin's Press, 1995.

Wilkerson, Tichi, and Marcia Borie. *Hollywood Legends*. Los Angeles: Tale Weaver Publishing, 1988.

Index

$\mathcal{D}$

$\mathcal{E}$

Entertainment Tonight, 4
Evita, 49–51

F

Falcon Crest, 48, 95, 96, 98,
    100–103, 128, 194
Fisher, Carrie, 207
Fleming, Rhonda, 162
Ford, Henry, 26
40 Carats, 24, 27, 75
Fourth Estate, 94

G

Gardner, Ava, 137, 148–152
Garland, Judy, 131,
    145–146
Geisler, Jerry, 188–89, 190–
    91, 215
Gish, Lillian, 152
Glenby Corporation, 23
Grable, Betty, 8, 131, 132,
    145, 146, 154
Grant, Cary, 53, 122
Grant, Hugh, 4
Granville, Bonita, 146
Grey, Virginia, 145, 153

H

Hauer, Rutger, 122

Hays, Will, 132
Hayworth, Rita, 8, 100
Hearst newspaper chain, 68
Henie, Sonja, 139
Henner, Marilu, 122
Hiller, Arthur, 86
Holmby Hills, 201
Honolulu, 75–76
Horne, Lena, 35, 146, 151
Hotel Royale, 90
Hughes, Howard, 134–35
Hunter, Ross, 126
Hurt, William, 17

I

I. Magnin Department Store,
    23
Imitation of Life, 5, 27, 113–
    15, 126, 215
Ivory Tower, 8, 18–22, 195
    as a place of reclusion, 9,
    44
    price paid for, 126

J

Jewel auction, 218–19
Jimmy's, 85
Johnny Eager, 133

K

Kelly, Grace, 8
Kennedy, Rose, 26, 36